501 TV-free Party Games for Kids

Cover Design: Sam Grimmer
Typesetting: Palmer Higgs, Box Hill, Victoria, Australia

 Published in 2005 by Hinkler Books Pty Ltd
17–23 Redwood Drive
Dingley VIC 3172 Australia
www.hinklerbooks.com

ISBN 1 7412 1868 3
Printed and bound in Australia

TABLE OF CONTENTS

HOW TO USE THIS BOOK

501 Party Games for Kids gives you all the ideas and advice you need to ensure your child's next party is full of fun and full of surprises. Want exciting and individual invitation and costume ideas? Want novel decoration and cake tips? Want party games that will wow toddlers through to teenagers, no matter where their interests lie? Just choose a party theme that inspires and is appropriate for your child's age, and off you go!

Many of the suggested decorations, costumes, games and activities make use of everyday items you'll have laying around the house. Other items can be sourced inexpensively at $2-type shops, second-hand stores, newsagents, supermarkets and craft or department stores.

For easy reference, this book contains a Table of Contents at the beginning and an alphabetical index at the end. It is divided into the following categories.

SLEEPOVER PARTIES
ARTY PARTIES
MYSTERY AND MAGIC PARTIES
FOOD PARTIES
WORLD TRAVELLER PARTIES
SCIENCE AND NATURE PARTIES
CRAZY CIRCUS PARTIES
DRAMA PARTIES
MUSIC PARTIES
CAMPING AND SCAVENGER PARTIES
SAND AND WATER PARTIES
SPORTS AND GAMES PARTIES
BUGS, BEARS AND STORYBOOK PARTIES

The book has parties for children of all ages—from two-year-olds to teenagers. There will be something that is exactly right for your child. The suggested age range on each party is a guide only—remember that all kids are different and you'll soon know if an activity is too easy or too difficult for your child and their friends.

Many of the games in this book encourage learning and imaginative play, and parental involvement will see that the kids get the most out of it. But, just as importantly, it gives you all an opportunity to celebrate and have fun!

GUIDE TO SYMBOLS

This simple legend of symbols gives a quick visual reference to the basic elements present in each activity.

Outdoor Activity:
This symbol indicates an outdoor activity.

Indoor Activity:
This symbol indicates an indoor activity.

Note: If both symbols are ticked, the activity can be enjoyed both outdoors and indoors.

Adult Participation: This activity requires some degree of adult supervision or involvement. Read the party descriptions carefully to ascertain the degree of monitoring and participation required.

Pencils, Paints and Paper: This activity requires the basic drawing or painting tools. It can be as simple as a pencil and paper for keeping score in a game or more art materials for decorating etc.

Tools Required: This activity requires tools of some type. This could be anything from a simple bowl and vegetable peeler to balloons and craft materials. All these activities have been designed with the basic everyday items found in the home such as cereal boxes etc. Some activities may require items to be purchased from a shop but should be inexpensive or alternatives can be found.

Learning and Imagination: Just about all of the activities in this book encourage imaginative play and many contain important learning skills designed for fun. If the activity is simply a game to occupy a bored child this symbol will not be ticked.

The symbols indicated in this book are a guide only. It is the responsibility of all adults to determine the appropriate activities for each child and the skills they possess. The use of tools requires adult supervision.

Sleepover Parties

Pyjamas, slippers and pillows are just a
few props needed for these thrilling
night-time parties.

Ages 4–14

Fabulous Fashions

Whether you dress up in designer clothes or model the latest sleepwear, make a fashion statement at a Fabulous Fashions slumber party!

Invitations

- Buy paper dolls or make some out of stiff poster board.

- Photocopy pictures of all the kids.

- Cut out the heads and glue them onto the heads of the dolls.

- Draw plain white pyjamas or nightgowns for the paper dolls, photocopy them and cut them out, leaving tabs to secure to the dolls.

- Write party details on the back of each doll and ask guests to decorate the paper pyjamas and bring them to the party.
- At the party, award prizes for the paper pyjamas, such as Most Colourful, Strangest, Funniest, Most Creative and so on.

Prizes and Party Bags

- Fashion accessories, such as scrunchies, scarves, hair ribbons, hats, socks and so on
- Small personalised mirrors
- Fashion magazines

Glove Cakes

- Make cakes with white sponge and favourite fillings.
- Cut into glove shapes using a cookie cutter or sharp knife.
- Attach lollies to sponge fingers. If you like, make cuffs from whipped cream.

Costumes

- Ask each guest to bring a favourite fancy outfit, pyjamas, robe, slippers and any accessories that might be fun to share and wear, such as hats, shoes, costume jewellery and so on.
- The guests will also need form-fitting attire (tights, bike shorts or tank tops).

Decorations

- Drape one wall of the party room with sheets. Hang another set of sheets from the ceiling or a rope to create a curtain, leaving an opening for the models to walk through.
- Create a stage and runway using long lengths of red or white fabric, or several sheets of plywood.
- Collect lights from around the house—lamps, torches and so on—and set them up in the party room to spotlight the runway and stage.
- Set the table with makeup and a small mirror at each place and make a centrepiece using fashion accessories.
- Play disco music while guests model their outfits.

Games

1 Pair up the guests, then have them sit in a circle. Set out a large selection of dress-up clothes, including dresses, hats, tops, skirts, shawls, scarves, jewellery, socks and shoes. Select a pair of players and blindfold one of them. The blindfolded player is the Designer; the other is the Model. To make dressing the Model easier, the Model should wear tights and a tank top or other form-fitting attire. At the word 'Go!' the Designer has three minutes to select from the clothing pile and dress the model from head to foot—without looking! The Model can only stand still and cannot help the Designer with the dressing. When time is up, remove the blindfold and view the Model's new look! Take a picture, then repeat with other pairs.

2 Collect a few dozen scarves, buy some from a local second-hand shop, or make your own from silky fabric cut into lengths. Pile the scarves in the centre of the room. At the word 'Go!' the players may take one scarf at a time and design an outfit for themselves. They have five minutes to create their outfits. The player with the most complete outfit wins a prize. The rest win prizes for Funniest, Weirdest and so on.

3 At a second-hand shop, buy a variety of mismatched clothes and accessories, such as hats, shoes, wraps, tops, skirts, pants, jackets, wigs, jewellery and so on. Or raid your own wardrobes and borrow from friends and family. Have the Designers mix and match items to make unique fashion statements. Put on a fashion show by modelling the outfits on the stage and runway. Take turns playing Announcer and describing the outfits for the audience, for example: 'Leah is wearing a lovely sequined halter top with a square-dance skirt and combat boots ...'

4 Assemble an ample supply of tissue paper, crepe paper and toilet paper in a variety of colours and set the supplies in the middle of the party room along with tape and staplers. Or use fabric remnants instead of paper products. Pair up the guests and choose a Designer and Model in each pair. Have the Designers use the provided materials to create fashions on the Models. When everyone finishes, have the Models model the creations for everyone. Switch roles and repeat so everyone gets a chance to be a Designer and a Model.

5 Buy a pair of cute socks for each guest and tuck a small gift into each pair. Hide the socks with the gifts in them throughout the room. Give each of the guests one of the remaining socks and tell them that the matching socks have surprises inside. Then set them hunting!

6 Have everyone stand in a circle. Choose someone to be the Dancer and have that person stand in the centre. Then start the music. The Dancer must make up a dance for everyone to imitate. Change the music and the Dancer, until everyone has made up a dance.

Ages 4–14

Pillow Pals

Have all the Pillow Pals come share in the slumber fun!

Invitations

- Buy or make paper dolls.
- Gather photos of all the guests, cut out the outline of each guest's head, and glue each cut-out over the head of a different paper doll.
- Place the paper dolls in various positions, such as standing, sitting, doing a flip, or lying down, and glue them onto a large sheet of paper.
- Draw appropriate background details, such as sleeping bags, stuffed animals and snacks.
- Draw speech balloons and write in party details.
- Make a photocopy of the invitation for each guest; mail in large envelopes.

Pillow Cake

- Bake a rectangular cake, ice and place marshmallows around the edges.

Prizes and Party Bags

- Pillow Pals
- Pillowcases signed with guests' names
- Cartoon pillowcases
- Decorative throw pillows

Costumes

- Ask guests to bring pillows, sleeping bags, stuffed animals and white pillowcases (or you provide the pillowcases).

Decorations

- Collect pillows and place them around the room.
- Buy fun pillows with funny faces on them or shaped like animals. Set them around the room.
- Set a small pillow at each place setting.

Games

7 You can't have a Pillow Pals party without having a pillow fight! Arm each guest with a pillow, remove all breakables from the room, then let the battle begin! To keep control, call a time-out every few minutes so the players can rest.

8 Clear a large area or move everyone outdoors. Choose one player to be It and give her a pillow. Have her chase the other players and try to tag one of them with the pillow. Whoever gets tagged becomes It.

9 Lay pillows half a metre apart across the floor. Have each player try to walk from one side of the room to the other by stepping only on the pillows.

10 On one side of a large box, cut out a hole just a little larger than the fattest pillow. Have the players try to toss their pillows through the hole.

11 Remove the pillowcases from the pillows. Have the players step into them and pull them up as high as they will go. Line up the players along one wall and have them hop to the other side of the room. The first player to reach the other side wins a prize.

12 Have everyone stand in a circle. Give one player a pillow and have them quickly toss it to the player next to them. Keep adding pillows at regular intervals. When someone drops a pillow, start the game over. Work toward tossing around all the pillows!

13 Have each guest insert a sheet of cardboard into their white pillowcase and lay the pillowcase on the table. Provide permanent markers, fabric paints, puff paints, iron-on decals and other decorative items. Have the guests decorate their pillowcases to look like people or animals. When everyone finishes, have them slip the pillowcases onto their pillows and show off their new pals. Be sure to have them name their Pillow Pals!

14 Set a pillowcase for each guest on the table. Have guests sit around the table. Ask each guest to pass their pillowcase to the guest on their left. Have each guest sign their name on the pillowcase in front of them. Have the guests keep passing around the pillowcases until each guest signs every pillowcase.

15 Gather photos of each guest. Take them to a photocopy shop and have iron-on transfers made of the faces. Enlarge the photos, if necessary. Let guests iron their faces onto the middle of their pillowcases. Have them draw frames around their faces with permanent markers or puff paint.

Silly Olympics

The Silly Olympics are always held during slumber parties! Let the games begin!

Invitations

- For each guest, cut out a pair of orange-sized circles from white poster board.
- Buy red-white-and-blue ribbon, and cut a length 30 to 38 centimetres long.
- Loop the ribbon and glue ends onto one of the circles.

- Glue a length of red-white-and-blue rickrack or narrow, gathered ribbon to the edge of the same circle, leaving some to stick out all around.
- Glue the other circle on top, flush with bottom circle.
- Write a guest's name on the medallion in fancy 3D lettering.
- Decorate using red and blue pens but leave some areas white.
- Write the party details on the back of the medallion; mail in a large envelope.

Olympic Cake

- Prepare a large bowl of vanilla ice cream, covered with sliced strawberries and blueberries, and topped with whipped cream and a cherry.

Prizes and Party Bags

- Flag pillowcases
- Power snacks
- Sweatbands
- Olympic flags and medallions
- Chocolate medals wrapped in gold foil
- Pocket games

Costumes

- Ask the guests to wear tracksuits or shorts and T-shirts. Greet guests with forehead and wrist sweatbands, and give them scrunchies for their hair.

Decorations

- Make a welcome sign that reads 'Silly Olympics Stadium' and the date.
- Tape Australian flags or flags from other countries to the walls.
- Drape coloured streamers from the centre of the ceiling to the walls.
- Tape posters of Olympic athletes to the walls.
- On a table, set bottled water, power drinks, power snacks, band-aids, wrist wraps, ice packs and so on.
- Play marching band music.

Games

16 Have the players step into their sleeping bags and line up along one wall. At the word 'Go!' have them hop across the room. If a player falls, he or she has to return to the starting line and start over. Change the races so the players must hop backward, hop sideways, roll sideways or inchworm on their tummies—all inside their sleeping bags!

17 Set up an obstacle course throughout the room. For example, stack pillows, line up chairs, set out a table, lay a plank across two sawhorses and so on. Have the players get inside their sleeping bags and take turns manoeuvering through the course. Time each player and present a prize for the fastest course completion. For added fun, have the players set up their own courses for each other.

18 Spread the sleeping bags on the floor. Choose one player to be It. Have him or her leave the room. Have each player get inside a sleeping bag other than their own and cover up completely except for one body part. Have It return to the room and guess who is in each sleeping bag just by looking at the exposed body part. Let each guest take a turn being It.

19 Divide the group into two teams. Give each team a sleeping bag. See how many teammates each team can fit inside its sleeping bag!

20 For each player, provide a different large object, such as a pillow, shoe box, stuffed animal, brick, rolled-up newspaper, pair of shoes and so on. Have the players leave the room and hide an item inside each sleeping bag. Have the players return to their sleeping bags. At the word 'Go!' have them feel the outside of their sleeping bags and try to guess what's inside. The first player to identify her item wins a prize—maybe what's inside the bag!

21 Select one player and have the others leave the room. The player must hide an alarm clock inside one of the sleeping bags and set it to go off in one minute. When the players return, they have 60 seconds to find the alarm clock just by listening for the ticking! Repeat until everyone has a turn hiding the alarm clock.

22 Give each guest a white pillowcase. Set out materials for decorating the pillowcases, such as permanent markers, fabric paints, puff paints and so on. Have the guests design their own Silly Olympics Flags.

23 Set out a white poster board, markers, glitter, sequins, trim, ribbons and so on. Have the guests make their own medallions for the games. If you prefer, award a medallion for each guest for every event, a blue one for the first-place winner, a red one for the second-place winner, and white ones for everyone else.

24 In the morning, award medallions for Best Laugh, Loudest Snorer, Floor-Space Hog, Longest Awake, Earliest to Fall Asleep, First Up and so on.

Ages 6–14

PJ Party

If you want to host a PJ Party—day or night—all your guests need is sleepwear! Once they're dressed for bed, keep them wide awake with lots of sleepy-time games and activities!

Invitations

- Photocopy and cut out pictures of your guests, using snapshots borrowed from parents. Fold paper into a side-fold card. Open the card and place a cut-out head near the top, leaving room for a body. Dress the body in pyjamas by cutting out a pyjama shape from a piece of flannel fabric and gluing it underneath the head. Close the card and cut out a hole in front to reveal the child's face. Write 'You're invited …' on the outside of the card, and '… to a PJ Party!' on the inside, along with the party details. Mail to guests.

Cereal Pillow Cake

- Bake a rectangular cake; cool.
- Cover the cake with fluffy white icing so it looks like a soft pillow.
- Crush a cup or two of colourful sweetened cereal and sprinkle over the Pillow Cake.

Prizes and Party Bags

- Send the sleepyheads home with tiny teddy bears.
- Give the kids new toothbrushes to use at home.
- Hand out small pillows or pairs of sleep socks to go with the kids' PJs.

Costumes

- Ask your guests to dress in sleepwear—pyjamas, long johns, robes and slippers.
- Tell the guests that teddy bears, blankets, pillows and other sleeping accessories are also welcome.

Decorations

- Set up the party room to look like a giant sleeping area.
- Spread out mattresses, or cover the floor with sheets, blankets and lots of pillows. Host the party right in the middle of the giant 'bed'.
- Keep the lights dim.

- Play lullabies for background music.
- Hang up pictures of people who are sleeping or are dressed in pyjamas.
- Set teddy bears and other sleepy-time items around the party room.

Games

25 Play the Slipper Game. Put all the guests' slippers into a pile. When you say 'Go!' have the kids race to see who can locate and put on his or her slippers first.

26 Play the Slipper Game again, but this time blindfolded. Have each guest, one at time, feel the slippers and try to guess which ones are his or hers.

27 Play Hide the Slippers. Tuck the slippers into nooks and crannies around the party room. Let the guests try to find them in a kind of treasure-hunt game.

28 Set out all the slippers in a row, and have the kids match the slippers to the guests.

29 Have the kids close their eyes, pass the slippers around in a circle and identify their owner just by feel.

Ages 8–14

Wake-up Party

This is a surprise party, but not for the guest of honour. It's a surprise for the invited guests! And even better—it happens at the crack of dawn, so the kids come as they are! This party is truly a wake-up call that will get the kids 'up 'n at 'em!'

Invitations

- You won't need invitations, since the guests don't know they are invited to a party! But you do have to let the parents know ahead of time. Call the parents when you think the invited guests aren't around and explain the party details. Tell them what day and time you're coming to wake up the kids—and that they are NOT to tell them. Ask the parents to have robes and slippers ready.

- If you prefer, send an invitation to the guests to let them know a party is being planned, but tell them the date and time are a surprise!

Sunshine Cake

- Set a cluster of cinnamon rolls together to form a large circle.
- Decorate the rolls with yellow-tinted cream icing.
- Make a face on the sun using cut-up fruit.

Prizes and Party Bags

- Give the kids personalised toothbrushes to take home.
- Let the kids take home the makeup and hair products they used.

Costumes

- Pyjamas, of course. Tell the kids to come to the party in their sleeping clothes, robes and slippers.
- If the kids' pyjamas aren't appropriate to be worn outside the house, let the kids put on another layer, but don't let them change!
- Have the guest of honour also wear pyjamas while collecting all the guests.

Decorations

- Decorate the dining room or kitchen to look like an early-morning café.
- Cut out a big yellow sun to greet the guests at the front door.

- Make 'Good Morning' posters. Write 'Good Morning' in several different languages on sheets of paper and hang the posters on the walls.
- Drape the ceiling in yellow and orange crepe paper and dangle personalised toothbrushes from the centre.
- Place bright yellow balloons around the party room to help wake up the kids.

Games

30 Bring along a tape recorder as you wake the kids and tape the scene. Play back the tape at the party and see if everyone can guess who's being awakened.

31 Set out a number of morning items, such as a toothbrush, a newspaper, a coffee cup and a cereal box and have the kids study the items for one minute. Remove the items and see how many items the kids can recall.

32 Go around the circle and have each player name one item. Let that player keep the item he or she named.

33 Model nightware for one another, and put on a pyjama fashion show, complete with a narrator who can point out the fashion statements in detail.

34 Have a pyjama parade down the street!

Ages 8–14

Friends Forever

What better way to celebrate friendship than at a Friends Forever slumber party?

Invitations

- Photocopy photos of each guest from snapshots.
- Cut out outlines of the guests. Arrange then glue them in a group setting onto a sheet of paper.
- Make a photocopy of the group picture for each guest.
- Glue the group picture in the centre of a sheet of light-coloured poster board to make a frame. Write party details on the back.
- Decorate the frame using stickers, puff paints and markers.
- Mail or hand-deliver in a large padded envelope.

Spell-your-name Mini Cakes

- Provide alphabet cookie cutters and refrigerate biscuit dough.
- Have the friends cut out letters of their names with cookie cutters.
- Bake the biscuits, then have the friends spell out their names and eat!
- Or have the friends make up nicknames for each other and cut out letters to spell them.

Prizes and Party Bags

- Scrapbooks
- Personalised pillowcases
- Friendship bracelets
- Framed Polaroid snapshots
- Poster-size photos of friends

Decorations

- Take Polaroid snapshots of guests as they arrive and glue them onto paper frames. Tape them to the walls.

- Hang a banner at the front door that reads 'Welcome Friends' in several different languages. Write guests' names on the banner. Decorate the banner with markers, stickers, puff paints, glitter, streamers and other decorating items. Have the guests try to identify each language.

- Set out friendship items on the table, such as bracelets, autograph books, photo books, scrapbooks and mementos.

- Enlarge the group picture made for the invitations. Make copies to use for place mats and wall posters.

Games

35 Make a list of categories, such as favourite colour, TV show, song, movie star, shop, holiday spot, teacher and so on. Make a copy of the list for each friend. Have the friends fill in their favourites under each category and sign their names. Collect all the lists. Read one list of favourites but not the writer's name. When finished, have the friends guess the writer of the list. For more excitement, read one favourite category at a time, and have the friends immediately guess the identity of the writer. Keep reading favourites until someone guesses correctly.

36 Give each friend a pad and pencil. Have them write down their most embarrassing moment. Collect all the pads, then read them one at a time and let the friends guess whose embarrassing moment it was. At the end of the game, vote who had the most embarrassing moment and award that friend a prize. Some appropriate prizes might be posters of passé pop stars, deodorant and so on.

37 Interview each guest before the party and write down their answers to personal questions like 'Where were you born', 'What is your favourite vegetable', 'Who was your first crush', 'What time do you go to bed', 'What kind of car do you want', 'What do you want to be when you grow up', 'What did you do on your holiday last year'. Use the answers to create game questions, such as 'Who was born in Germany', 'Whose first crush was Tommy', 'Who loves spinach', and so on. Read the questions one at a time, and have the guests guess the correct friend.

38 Draw a ten-by-ten-square grid on poster board to make a playing card; make enough cards for everyone. Cover the cards with clear contact paper or laminate them. Distribute the cards along with wipe-off felt-tip pens. Choose one player, then have everyone write as much of his or her full name as will fit in the first row, leaving the first square blank. Have everyone brainstorm and write the same nine categories down the left column, such as 'chocolate bars', 'rock stars', 'boys' names', 'colours', 'animals', 'song titles', 'clothing', 'body parts' and 'games', one subject in each square, leaving the first square blank. Set a timer for three minutes and have players race to fill in the squares with words that fit the categories on the side and begin with the letters at the top. When time is up, the player with the most filled-in squares wins a prize. Have the players wipe off the squares with tissues or rags and write another player's name at the top. They can use the same categories listed down the left side or make up new ones.

39 Provide lots of coloured embroidery string and beads and have the friends make friendship bracelets. Have everyone write their names on slips of paper and place the slips into a bowl. Each friend draws a name out of the bowl and gives her bracelet to that person. Keep drawing names and exchanging bracelets.

40 Buy a scrapbook for each guest, or have them make their own by covering two sheets of 20 × 30 centimetre cardboard with decorative contact paper or glued fabric. Insert plain white paper between the covers, punch holes on the left side through all the layers and tie together with colourful ribbon. Provide stickers, coloured markers and pens, diecuts, punches, stamps and other decorative items. Provide teen magazines, holiday brochures and so on. Let the friends take Polaroid snapshots of each other. Have the friends fill their scrapbooks with the snapshots, friendship items brought from home and the provided materials.

41 Provide a plain, long, white or pastel T-shirt for each friend. Let the kids pass the T-shirts around and sign their names with permanent markers or puff paints. Have them decorate with fabric paints, iron-on decals, embroidery string and so on. Have the friends sleep in their Friendship Nightshirts.

42 Play the Robe Game. Pair up the kids and have one player in each pair put on a robe. Have the pairs hold hands. The person wearing the robe must try to remove it and get it onto the second person, without letting go of his or her hands.

43 Play Blanket Ball. Spread out a blanket and have all the guests stand around the edge of the blanket and hold a piece of it. Toss a ball into the centre and have the players keep the ball bouncing by moving the blanket up and down. (You may want to do this outside. If not, remove all breakables!)

44 Have the kids do each other's hair and makeup. Tell ghost stories or watch a scary video. Play board games.

45 Design new sleepwear fashions.

46 Play Truth or Dare. Have everyone confess to a secret in answer to a question. Those who don't confess have to face the consequences, such as 'Sing opera', 'Dance the twist', or 'Count backwards from 100'.

47 Tie a ribbon to the toes of the kids who fall asleep and connect the ribbon to other sleepy toes in the room.

48 Let the kids carve their own snow people from Styrofoam.

49 Have the kids make individual ice-cream sculptures. They can eat their works of art.

50 Make 'snowballs' out of wadded up white paper and cotton balls, or balled white socks. Toss them around the room. (Make sure to remove all breakables.)

51 Make snowballs by scooping out balls of vanilla ice cream and rolling them in flaky coconut.

52 Make your own snow cones using real snow. Get a scoop of snow, pour some juice on top, and eat. Make snow by whirling ice in a blender.

53 Make penguins by cutting open dates, filling with cream cheese to make tummies and adding tiny cheese triangles for beaks and feet.

Arty Parties

These parties will stimulate kids'
creativity and have them amused for
hours!

Ages 2–6

Toon Town Party

Move into Toon Town for a party full of animated fun. Have your child choose his or her favourite comic or cartoon character and use it as your theme for everything—from invitations to favours. When the kids see Mickey, Minnie, Bugs or Popeye at the party, they'll go Looney Tunes!

Invitations

- Make one copy of a favourite cartoon character for each guest. Fold the sheets of paper into invitations, and make speech bubbles inviting the kids to the party.

- Create a cartoon character with the body of Mickey Mouse or Bugs Bunny and the head of an invited guest! Make photocopies of the character and of the guest photo, cut and paste onto a card and you've got a personalised Toon Town invitation.

Cartoon Character Cake

- Buy a cartoon cake mould at a party store, or make a cartoon shape yourself with some creative carving. Easy faces to make include Mickey Mouse, Miss Piggy, Daffy Duck and Bart Simpson.

- Decorate the cake with white icing.
- Add details with piping bag.

Prizes and Party Bags

- Send the kids home with little plastic figurines of cartoon characters.
- Give the kids comic books.

Costumes

- Have the kids come dressed as their favourite cartoon character. On the invitation, give the kids lots of characters from which to choose, including Mickey Mouse, Bugs Bunny, Road Runner, Beavis and Butthead, Bart Simpson, Porky Pig, Sylvester the Cat, Tweety Bird, Animaniacs and so on.

Decorations

- Tape cut-outs of cartoon characters all around the room.
- Use comic books as place mats.
- Hang posters of your kid's favourite cartoon critters on the walls.
- Place small plastic figures of cartoon characters on the table to form a centrepiece.
- Use lots of balloons to fill the room with colour, and draw cartoon faces on each of the balloons.

Games

54 Play Name That Cartoon. Have the kids listen to cartoon jingles and guess the name of the shows.

55 Cover up cartoon characters and let the kids peek at just the eyes or mouths of characters and try to guess who they are.

56 Have the kids act out cartoon characters while the others try to guess the characters.

57 Cut pictures of cartoon characters into puzzle pieces. Have the kids race to assemble their puzzles.

58 To make the puzzle game harder, put all the puzzle pieces into one big pile, and have the kids find the pieces that belong to their puzzle.

59 Let the kids create their own cartoon characters, complete with costumes and funny names. Have the kids use crepe paper and second-hand shop accessories, such as jewellery, hats, gloves, vests, jackets, shoes and wigs, to create the costumes.

60 Have the kids make a giant cartoon panel. Have the kids draw cartoon characters on square sheets of white paper. Then have them fill in speech bubbles, saying something about the pictures. Line the pictures along the wall and read the cartoon panel from start to finish. Enjoy the silly story.

61

Supply the kids with cut-up veggies and fruits and a variety of spreads, and let them make open-face cartoon sandwiches on white bread.

Ages 4–12

Crafty Artists Party

Let the kids create their own party with a Crafty Artists Party! All you need are art supplies—paints, crayons, paper and glue—to give your gathering a creative start in art. Everything, from the invitations to the favours, is sure to be a masterpiece!

Invitations

- Send your guests Magic Rainbow invitations. Completely cover white postcard with different colours of crayons. Paint over the crayons with black poster paint. When the paint is dry, scratch off the party details using an opened paper clip. Watch the colourful words appear under the black paint.

Artists Palate Cake

- Bake enough cupcakes for all the guests; cool.
- Tint white icing with food colouring to create a variety of colours. Cover each cupcake with a different colour icing.
- Cut out an artist's palate from poster board. Arrange the cupcakes in a three-quarter circle on top of the palate and place in the centre of the table.

- Lay a few paint brushes nearby for effect.
- Or bake a rectangular cake and let the kids 'paint' the cake with small paint brushes and bowls of tinted icing.

Prizes and Party Bags

- Send the kids home with watercolour paint sets, crayons or colourful felt-tip pens.
- Give the kids any other art supplies so they can continue the creative process at home.
- Give the kids how-to-draw or colouring books.

Costumes

- Ask your guests to dress like artists and wear smocks.
- Provide old shirts for the kids to wear at the party. Inexpensive shirts are available at second-hand shops. Make the smocks look more authentic by adding little colour splashes using acrylic paints, felt-tip pens or puff paints.
- Give each child a beret to wear with his or her outfit.

Variations

- Take the kids to an art class or studio and watch the artists create their work.
- Ask the instructor to include the kids in an art or craft activity.
- Visit an art museum that features art that appeals to kids.

Helpful Hints

- Crafty Artists parties are messy—but that's half the fun. Be sure to cover the party area with newspapers and drop cloths so you won't have to worry about the mess.

- Attach strings to paint brushes and have the kids wear the paint brush necklaces around their necks. (Make sure to carefully supervise young guests. Necklaces can pose a strangulation risk to small children.)

Decorations

- Set up easels, craft areas and art supplies, including paints, crayons, felt-tip pens, clay, wood, stencils, glitter, sequins, ribbon, glue, tape, stapler, scissors and string.
- Cut out paper frames and stack them along walls. Use the frames to frame the kids' artwork during the party.
- Cover the table with a white sheet of paper, and let the kids decorate their own tablecloth with the art supplies.
- Hang up prints of famous artists to inspire the kids' creativity.

Games

62 Play Pass the Portrait. Give each child a sheet of white paper lined into eight horizontal sections. Have each kid draw a face on the top section, then fold back the section with the head and pass it to the next player. Tell them to draw a neck and shoulders, without looking at the head. Fold back the next section, hiding the shoulders, and continue passing the papers until the entire body has been drawn, piece by piece. Unfold the

portraits to see the funny results! Have the guests name the portraits and hang them on the walls. (If you prefer, pass around one sheet at a time.)

63 Have the kids use art materials to create works of art. Frame and display the finished products. Give everyone an award for creativity.

64 Finger-paint with vanilla custard tinted with food colour, so the kids can taste-test their work as they create a picture.

65 Show the kids how to decorate T-shirts with puff paints and permanent felt-tip pens.

66 Make Baker's Clay by combining four cups of flour, one cup of salt and one and a half cups of water. Let the kids make whatever they want, then bake the dough in the oven at 120°C for one hour, or until firm. Paint the clay creations when they're cool.

67 Serve painted sandwiches by letting the kids 'paint' on white bread slices with food colouring. Then toast the bread to make it firm.

68 Have the kids design their own crafty snacks from peanut butter playdough by mixing one cup of smooth peanut butter with half a cup of honey, and one cup of non-fat dry milk. Let the kids play with the dough for a while, then let them eat it when they are finished. (Make sure that everyone washes their hands before playing with the dough, so they don't eat any glue or glitter!)

Ages 4–14

Arty Party

Showcase your guests' creative talents with an awesome Arty Party!

Invitations

- Photocopy pictures of the guests.
- Colour each copy with felt-tip pens and coloured pencils. Make the invitations look interesting, not necessarily realistic!
- Cut a small frame from poster board and glue the coloured copy inside.
- Glue two small sticks on the back of the portrait in an inverted V shape, with the legs sticking out out the bottom to look like an easel.
- Write party details on the frame.
- Mail each guest her own portrait in a padded envelope.

Rainbow Parfait Cakes

- Buy a rainbow variety of sorbet flavours, such as raspberry, orange, lemon, lime and grape.
- Buy plastic parfait glasses, rent them at a party store, or use tall, clear drinking glasses.
- Place a scoop of sorbet at the bottom of each glass, then add a little whipped cream.
- Add another flavour of sorbet and another dollop of whipped cream. Repeat until the glass is filled with a rainbow of sorbet.
- Top with a dollop of whipped cream and a cherry.
- Stick a small, stiff, clean, new paint brush into each concoction and let the kids eat their parfait cakes with the brushes for fun.

Prizes and Party Bags

- Art supplies
- Drawing pads
- Art instruction books
- Craft kits
- Colourful smocks
- Art books for kids

Costumes

- Ask the artists to bring smocks to wear over their clothes. Provide scrunchies or headbands to tie back loose hair. Ask guests to bring art materials to share.

Decorations

- Line one wall with several large sheets of white paper connected together. Create a mural during the party.

- Cut frames from poster board and tape them to the walls.
- Tape posters of famous paintings to the walls for inspiration.
- Set art supplies on the table for easy access. If using paints, provide plenty of clean rags and bowls of water to wipe and rinse paintbrushes.
- Make a tablecloth from butcher paper. Draw a picture frame at each place setting, then have the guests draw their own faces inside the frames and decorate the frames with glitter, sequins, markers and other craft items.
- Create flowers from colourful pipe cleaners. Poke the stems into a block of Styrofoam covered with green tissue paper. Use as a centrepiece.
- Cover the entire floor with a drop cloth, then set up easels, worktables and a variety of art and craft stations.

Games

69 Write the name of each guest on a strip of paper. Sit the guests in a circle and give each a drawing pad, a pencil and a name strip, making sure everyone gets someone else's name. Tell the artists they have ten minutes to draw portraits of the people whose names they have. When the portraits are complete, have the artists hold up their drawings one at a time as the rest of the group try to guess who it is. It won't be easy!

70 Find a familiar character. Have the artists sit in a circle with drawing pads and pencils. Choose one guest to be the Instructor, and have him or her look at the character. The Instructor must explain exactly what the artists should draw by telling them where to move their pencils ('Draw straight up 25 millimetres. Then back down. Then over to the right . . .'). The artists are not allowed to ask any questions. After the Instructor finishes giving directions, have the artists display their drawings one at a time. Then reveal the character and compare it with the drawings. Repeat with different Instructors and characters.

71 Seat the guests on the floor in a circle. Place drawing pads and pencils flat on the floor in front of them. Set an object, such as a bowl of fruit, a teddy bear or an article of clothing, in the centre of the circle. Ask the artists to remove their footwear and draw the object with one foot. When everyone finishes, take a vote on the best picture and award the artist a blue ribbon. (To make the game more challenging, limit the drawing time.)

72 Prepare a stack of cards with words or phrases. Divide the group into two teams: Team A and Team B. Set a large pad of paper on an easel. Have a member of Team A pick a card and draw the word or phrase. If the other members of Team A guess the word or phrase in less than a minute, they get a point. Alternate between teams until all the cards are gone. The team with the most points wins the game.

73 Tape several large sheets of paper to the wall. Provide lots of art materials, such as felt-tip pens, crayons, watercolours, poster paints, glitter glue, magazine cut-outs, fabric pieces and so on. Have the group decide on a theme, such as 'Life of a School Kid', 'Today's Pop Music', Going on a Picnic', or 'Summer!' Place each guest at a section of the mural and ask them all to create artwork that goes with the theme. When everyone finishes, stand back and admire the mural. After everyone has studied the mural for a few minutes, ask the artists to explain how their sections tie in with the theme.

74 Buy one light-coloured plastic light switch plate for each guest. Provide stickers, adhesive letters, stamps, magazine cut-outs, lolly wrappers, acrylic paint, coloured tissue paper and so on. Let the guests decorate their light switch plates. When they finish, create a mixture of three parts of white glue and one part of warm water. Have the artists apply a coating of the diluted glue over their designs to preserve them. The kids can take home their light switch plates to use in their bedrooms.

Ages 8–12

Upside-down, Inside-out and Backwards Party

The kids will feel like Alice in Wonderland when they attend this upside-down, inside-out, and backwards party. Remember to do the opposite of what you usually do and you can't go wrong—er ... right! Now, 'don't' invite the guests and 'don't' have a good time! (Opposite!)

Invitations

- Write the party details on the backs of the invitations, and write the information upside down and backwards so your guests have to decipher it. Fold the cards inside out, and place them in the envelopes upside down. Address the backs of the envelopes, instead of the fronts. (Make sure you write the addresses correctly or they may not get there!)

Upside-down Cake

- Bake a packet mix pineapple upside-down cake, or use a favourite recipe.

- Use coloured alphabet noodles to write the kids' names backwards on the cake.

- Turn the cake out of the baking tin in front of the kids so they can see the surprise topping when you flip it upside down.

- Make upside-down ice cream sundaes to go with the cake. Begin with the toppings, and pile on the sundae ingredients until you end up with ice cream on top. Or, make inverted ice cream cones. Scoop balls of ice cream onto small plates, top with ice cream cones, and let the kids decorate the cones with piping bags to make clowns, monsters, or anything they like.

Prizes and Party Bags

- Give the kids mirrors so they can do backwards things at home.

- Offer the kids comic books, with the covers stapled on upside down.

- Let the kids take home the tornadoes in the bottles they made.

- Give the kids snowstorm jars that must be turned upside down to see the snow fall. You can buy these or make them yourself.

- Offer the kids anything that can be turned upside down, inside out, or backwards.

Costumes

- Ask the kids to dress in clothes they have put on inside out, upside down and backwards. They may arrive with their pants turned inside out, their shirts put on backwards and their socks worn over their shoes! Anything goes, as long as everything is put on strangely!

Variation

- Instead of an Upside-down, Inside-out and Backwards Party, host a Big/Little Party, in which everything is either very big or very little.

Helpful Hint

- Give 'tickets' to the kids every time they make a violation and don't do something upside down, inside out, or backwards. The player with the fewest tickets wins an upside-down prize!

Decorations

- Greet your guests facing backwards and tell them 'not' to come in.
- Hang posters upside down.
- Hang balloons by string from the ceiling so they appear upside down.
- Turn knick-knacks in the party room upside down.
- Set up the party food under the table, and have the kids sit on the floor—under the table—to enjoy the party treats.
- Set the cups and plates upside down and the silverware backwards.

Games

75 Play your favorite games—but with a twist: backwards!

76 Instead of pinning the tail on the donkey's rear, pin it on the nose!

77 Play musical chairs, but instead of finding a seat when the music stops playing, find one when it begins!

78 Have a bunch of relay races in the backyard and run them all backwards!

79 Have the kids dress normally, and choose one player to leave the room. While the player is gone, have one guest turn an article of clothing inside out, backwards or upside down. When the player returns, have him or her guess which guest made a change and what it was.

80 Try drawing backwards. Give guests sheets of paper and set them in front of a mirror. Place a picture facing the mirror and have the kids copy the picture without looking at it. They may look only in the mirror as a guide. See who can make the best drawing—it won't be easy!

81 Tell a round-robin story, but begin at the end and have the kids continue the story— backwards!

82 Make Tornadoes in a Bottle. Clean large plastic drink bottles and fill them three-quarters full with coloured water. Fill the rest of the bottle with oil and glitter. Seal the lid with glue. Have the kids swirl the bottles and turn them upside down to see the tornado.

83 Make inside-out sandwiches. Place the filling on top of the bread slices, instead of inside.

Ages 8–12

Time Machine Party

It's fun to rediscover old stuff that you've long forgotten. This time capsule party will transport the kids from the present to the past—but it won't happen until the future!

Invitations

- Write the party details on a scroll, burn the edges of the paper, roll it up, and tie it with a ribbon. Mail the scrolls in padded envelopes or hand-deliver to the kids.
- Borrow baby pictures of each guest, photocopy them several times and write the party details on the backs. Mail to guests.
- For added fun, make a collage of all the guests' baby pictures, and make copies to use as the invitations.

Time Cake

- Bake a round cake according to packet directions; cool.
- Decorate the cake with white icing.
- Using piping bags, draw the face of a clock, with the numbers and the hands.

- Use different coloured icing for the number that reflects the child's age (if making this cake for a birthday).

Prizes and Party Bags

- Give the kids baby bottles filled with jelly beans or other treats.
- Give each kid a diary to keep track of the upcoming year.
- Hand out scrapbooks so the kids can keep time capsules of their own over the years.

Costumes

- Ask the kids to bring something special from the past, such as blankets or teddy bears. Provide dummy necklaces and decorated juice bottles when the kids arrive.
- Have the kids come as they may look in the future.

Decorations

- Display baby items throughout the party room. Include bottles, nappies, dummies, baby equipment and so on. Borrow items from friends with babies if you don't have the items on hand.
- Check a poster store for funny baby pictures to hang on the walls and display baby pictures of the guests.
- Secretly borrow some old toys from the kids and feature them on the party table.

- Enlarge recent pictures of the kids, cut off the heads and paste the heads onto new bodies. It's fun to select actors and performers, such as Justin Timberlake and Britney Spears.

Games

84 Display the kids' baby pictures and have them try to guess who's who.

85 Find some baby pictures of Hollywood stars and have the kids try to guess their identities.

86 Put a bunch of baby items into paper bags and have the kids feel inside the bags to guess the items.

87 Hold up each item you've borrowed from guests' homes, and ask the others players to guess to whom the toys belong.

88 Put together a group time capsule. Have the kids decide what should go into the capsule. You might want to include a newspaper, a popular toy, a class picture, a comic book, an article of fad clothing and so on. Seal the items in a small metal box, and bury it in the backyard. Tell the kids you will all meet in five or ten years, dig up the box and see what's inside!

Trash Bash Party

Recycle the fun over and over again, with a Trash Bash celebration. Help save the planet as you party and come away with lots of homemade toys and games, all created from throwaways. The best part is—a Trash Bash doesn't cost a lot to host!

Invitations

- Use old newspapers to create your trash bash invitations. Hand print or use a computer to create an article with the party details. Make copies and cut-and-paste them into real newspaper pages. When the kids read the headlines, they'll find they're invited to a party!

- Send the invitations in envelopes made from recycled paper, of course.

Recycled Cupcakes

- Prepare cupcake mixture.
- Clean a variety of small cans, such as tuna, olive and tomato sauce. Remove all jagged edges.
- Spray the cans with vegetable spray.
- Pour cupcake mixture into the cans.

- Bake according to packet directions; cool.
- Decorate the cupcakes with chocolate and white icing, and top with sprinkles left over from old parties.
- Serve the cupcakes in the cans.

Prizes and Party Bags

- Give the kids recycled stationery.
- Send the kids home with the sock puppets.
- Give the kids fancy rubbish bins covered with contact paper or painted with flowers. Tell them to use them to recycle at home.
- Offer scarves made from old dresses purchased from a second-hand shop.
- Hand out 'collector boxes' made from recycled margarine tubs or other containers.

Costumes

- Ask the kids to dress creatively, using old junk in a new way. With a little recycled paper, cut-up plastic or clean cans, the guests can use their imaginations to create a whole new/old look!

Decorations

- Cover the party table with old newspaper.
- Serve drinks in a variety of clean plastic bottles, cans with smooth edges and other recyclables.

- Serve food on cleaned foil or plastic TV dinner trays.
- Get mismatched silverware from friends or a second-hand shop.
- Make a centrepiece out of old clean socks turned into puppets. Make one for each guest to take home at the end of the party.
- Place 'recycle' stickers around the room and on the guests as they arrive.

Games

89 Make a fun game from clean, plastic milk bottles. Cut off the tops, leaving the handles intact and give one to each guest. Have the kids toss a tennis ball back and forth between the scoops.

90 Make Squirt Birds from old plastic squirt bottles. Clean the bottles thoroughly, then let the kids draw funny faces on the tops of the bottles—birds, monsters or whatever they like. Add beaks or other details with pom-poms or plastic margarine-tub cutouts. Secure with a glue gun. Take the Squirt Birds outside and have a water war.

91 Make candle holders. Clean small cans, such as tuna or olive cans, and paint the cans with acrylic paint, or cover them with colourful contact paper. Fill with pieces of old or broken candles, fill in the spaces with paraffin wax add new wicks and you have new recycled candles!

92 Make sock puppets. Give the kids permanent felt-tip pens and have them draw eyes, noses and mouths on old socks. Slip the sock onto your hand and watch the puppet come to life.

93 Award prizes for costumes. Make sure every guest gets a prize by having lots of different categories, such as Most Interesting, Best Use of Plastic, Most Likely to Go Straight to the Tip and so on.

Ages 8–14

Creative Crafts

Host a make-it and take-it slumber party with lots of creative crafts to keep the sleepless crowd busy.

Invitations

- Preheat the oven to 180°C.

- With colourful permanent markers, write a message like 'Let's party!' in large letters on a Styrofoam dinner plate or a clean, dry Styrofoam meat tray. (Wash in a mild bleach solution to kill germs.) Decorate the plate or tray with pictures and/or designs.

- Use a pencil to poke a hole about 15 millimetres from the top edge of the plate or tray.

- Put the plate or tray face up on a baking sheet and place in oven for 45 to 60 seconds. The heat will make the Styrofoam curl and shrink, then flatten and harden.

- Remove shrunken pendant from oven and let cool on counter.

- While pendant cools, use a fine-point permanent marker to write party details on a length of ribbon.
- Thread ribbon through hole in pendant.
- Make one pendant invitation for each guest and mail in padded envelopes.

Peanut Butter Playdough Cake

- Mix 1 cup of peanut butter with ½ cup honey.
- Add ½ cup of instant non-fat dry milk (or more, as needed).
- Mix with hands to a dough-like consistency—not too dry or too sticky.

- Divide dough among guests and let them shape it into anything they like.
- Provide seeds, sultanas, shredded coconut and sprinkles for decoration.
- Let the artists eat their creations!

Prizes and Party Bags

- Craft kits
- Craft instruction books
- Decorated smocks
- Clay recipes and ingredients

Costumes

- Ask guests to bring any craft supplies they have, including old T-shirts to cover their clothes.

Decorations

- Cover worktables with newspapers or paper tablecloths.
- For inspiration, display finished samples of the crafts guests will be making.
- Set out a pair of scissors, tube of glue, set of markers and any other necessary materials for each guest.
- Make a centrepiece with craft materials. For example, attach paper flowers to paintbrushes and arrange them in an empty paint can. Add colourful markers, pencils and so on.

- If you already own any craft items, display them on boxes spray-painted gold. Attach outrageous price tags and give each item a silly, arty title.

Games

94 Use a large jar lid to trace a circle on a piece of cardboard; cut out the circle. Make a dot in the centre of the circle. Divide the circle into six wedges and colour the wedges red, orange, yellow, green, blue and purple. Make two small holes, one on each side of the centre dot, about 2½ cm apart. Thread a 1 metre length of string through both holes. Tie the ends to make two loops. Put one finger in each loop and twist the string by whirling the spinner like a jump rope. Now move your hands apart and together to make the circle spin. Watch the colours disappear and see who can spin their spinner the longest.

95 Buy an inexpensive unpainted pottery plate for each guest, a set of pottery paints and some brushes. Let guests paint their plates and sign their artwork. After the party have the plates fired at a pottery shop, then hand-deliver them to the guests.

96 Provide a small rectangle of clear glass or plastic for each guest. Let guests outline designs on their rectangles using black permanent markers. Have them paint inside the designs using glass paint. Wrinkle a large sheet of foil and flatten it out again. Then cut it into rectangles the size of the glass rectangles. Cut out black cardboard rectangles the same size. Lay the foil on top of the cardboard. Lay the glass on top of the foil, painted side down. Carefully press together. Wrap strong black tape around the edges of the pictures to frame them and hold them together. Attach a loop of fishing wire for hanging.

97 To make Baker's Clay, combine four cups of flour, one cup of salt and 1¾ cups of water in a bowl. Mix well. Divide the clay among the guests. Have each guest roll her dough into enough small beads to make a necklace. Poke toothpicks through beads to make holes. Leave the toothpicks in and place the beads on foil-covered baking sheets. Bake at 120°C for 30 to 60 minutes, until firm. Remove from oven, remove toothpicks, and let beads cool. Paint beads with poster paints and varnish for protection and shine. String beads onto elastic thread or coloured string, tie the ends together and wear.

98 Provide a plain white T-shirt for each guest. Let guests decorate their T-shirts with fabric paints.

Mystery and Magic Parties

These parties are spooky, mysterious and exciting. Perfect for kids who love a thrill!

Ages 6–12

Abracadabra Party

To create a magical Abracadabra Party, perform these amazing party-planning tricks that are sure to astound the kids. Then watch what appears right before your very eyes!

Invitations

- Write the party details on white cut-outs of a rabbit. Cut out a black hat and make a slit in the hat into which the rabbit 'disappears'. Leave the rabbit's ears showing, and let the kids pull the rabbits out of the hats to read the invitations.

- Write the party details with a white crayon on white paper to make the invitations appear blank. Include a colour crayon with each invitation and tell the guests to colour over the paper to magically reveal the party details!

Rabbit-in-a-hat Cupcakes

- Bake chocolate cupcakes according to packet directions; cool.

- Set each cupcake on top of an extra-large (about 12 centimetre) round chocolate biscuit to form a hat and brim. Place on individual plates.
- Roll vanilla ice cream balls in coconut.
- Add lolly eyes and nose to ice cream balls to make a rabbit face. Stick two triangle wafer cookies on top to make ears. (As you work on each ball, keep the rest frozen.)
- Set ice cream balls on top of cupcakes; serve to waiting magicians.

Prizes and Party Bags

- Send the budding magicians home with a collection of inexpensive magic tricks purchased from a toy store.
- Give the kids rabbits' feet for good luck.
- Hand out decks of cards so the kids can perform card tricks at home.
- Make magic wands by taping lengths of ribbon to wands and attaching a silver star cut from poster board to one end. Let the kids decorate their wands with pens, glue and glitter.

Variations
- Hire a professional magician to perform and teach magic tricks.
- Take the kids to a magic show to enjoy amazing tricks.

Helpful Hints
- Practice a few magic tricks yourself so you know they work well before you try them with the kids.
- Choose tricks that the kids can learn easily.

Costumes

- Ask the kids to come dressed as magicians, complete with capes and hats.
- Provide the kids with magic wands to complete their outfits.

Decorations

- Set up a stage in your party room where the kids can perform their magic acts. Spread a bright sheet or blanket over the floor to serve as the stage. Make a curtain from an old sheet and hang it from floor lamps or tall-backed chairs to hide behind-the-scenes preparations.
- Hang posters of great magicians, such as David Copperfield and Harry Houdini.
- Cut out classic symbols of magic, such as wands, hats and rabbits, from paper to decorate the walls.

Games

99 Play Mind Reader. Secretly select and coach a kid ahead of time to be the Mind Reader. When the game begins, 'randomly' select this child to be the Mind Reader. Ask the Mind Reader to leave the room, then select a Guilty Person. Have the Mind Reader return to the party. Ask the Mind Reader one question regarding the identity of the Guilty Person. 'Magically' the Mind Reader will identify the Guilty Person. Here's the trick: be sure to phrase the question using the Guilty Person's initials in the first two words. For example, if the Guilty Person is named Bruce Lansky, you might say, 'By looking around the room, can you tell us who is guilty'.

100 Spread out a number of magic tricks on the floor. Have the players close their eyes. Remove a trick. When the players open their eyes, they must guess which trick has disappeared. The player who correctly guesses the missing trick first wins the removed trick and drops out of the game. Continue until all the tricks have mysteriously vanished. (You may want to have enough tricks for all players, so everyone gets something.)

Ages 8–12

Sorcerer's Magic Party

With a few simple tricks, watch magic appear right before the guests' very eyes!

Invitations

- Buy a set of colour-changing markers that includes an invisible-ink pen. Buy a decoder pen for each guest.

- For each guest, draw a border of magic symbols, such as stars, question marks, or magic wands, along the edges of a sheet of white paper. Leave the centre of the sheet blank.

- Use an invisible-ink pen to write the party details inside the border.

- Wrap a note around a decoder pen instructing the guest to 'colour' the middle of the paper with the pen to reveal a magical message.

- Mail in a large envelope—don't forget to include the decoder pen!

Mini Card Cakes

- Make sandwiches with white bread and favourite fillings and spreads; cut off crusts.
- Cut each sandwich into two rectangles.
- Press biscuits shaped like hearts, diamonds, spades and clubs (available at gourmet stores, party stores and some grocery stores) in the centre of the top slice of each card cake.

Prizes and Party Bags

- Decks of playing cards or tarot cards.
- Simple magic tricks, such as the Coin Changer, the Finger Trap or the disappearing Coin.
- Books about magic tricks.
- Ask each guest to prepare a magic trick to perform at the party.

Decorations

- Cut out question mark shapes from white paper and paint them with glow-in-the-dark paint. Tape the question marks all over the ceiling and walls.
- Create a performance area by stringing rope from one wall to the opposite wall. Decorate a sheet with magic symbols and hang the sheet over the rope to make a curtain.
- Using double-sided tape, stick playing cards on the walls.

- Cover the table with a white sheet decorated with playing cards.
- Use a stuffed bunny in a magician's hat as a centrepiece.

Games

101 Before the party, ask a guest's parent to be the Psychic and explain to him or her the following trick. At game time, ask one guest to pick one playing card from a deck. Ask the guest to lay the card face up on the table. Tell the guests you are going to call the Psychic Hotline and the Psychic will guess the chosen card. Call the Psychic, and when he or she answers, follow this script:

Psychic: 'Hello?'

You: 'This is [your name].'

When the Psychic hears this, he or she counts from one to thirteen. You must interrupt when the Psychic reaches the number of the chosen card and ask, 'Is the Psychic there?'. The Psychic then knows the number of the chosen card. Now the Psychic recites the suits. You interrupt again when the Psychic says the correct suit and ask, 'Could you guess the card my guest selected?'. Then hold the phone out to the guests and have the Psychic loudly announce the chosen card to the amazement of all. Place a new call each time a player picks a card.

102 Choose one guest to be the Sorcerer. Turn off the lights and have everyone close their eyes. The Sorcerer should hide somewhere in the house. Leaving the lights off, give each guest a torch to try to find the Sorcerer and make him or her reappear.

103 Have the guests perform the tricks they brought from home in a Slumber Party Magic Show. Provide capes, top hats, magic wands and other appropriate costume accessories and props. When each guest finishes, have them reveal the secret of the trick. Teach the guests a few magic tricks you know (or learned before the party). Get some books on magic tricks and provide the necessary props to perform some selected tricks. Then let the group make more magic! Each magician should master at least one new trick.

104 Give each guest a large square of white fabric big enough to use as a cape. Provide glow-in-the-dark paints or markers. Let the guests decorate their capes. Then turn off the lights and have everyone creep around in their glowing capes!

105 Have one guest lie face up on a bed or couch with their head hanging off the end. Tie a scarf over the top half of their face so only their mouth and chin show. Use eyeliner to draw two eyes on their chin; add a moustache or lipstick. Have them act out a goofy skit with their new face.

Ages 8–12

Midnight Mystery

There's nothing mysterious about hosting a Midnight Mystery slumber party when all the clues to the fun are here!

Invitations

- Write a rough draft of your invitation, such as 'We're holding your party prize for ransom. Here's how to collect it …'
- From magazines, cut out the letters you'll need to spell out the invitation. Or use a ransom letter font available on some computer programs.
- Arrange the letter cut-outs into words and glue them onto a sheet of paper. (If you don't want to make a ransom invitation for each guest, make enough photocopies for the rest of the group, then colour the letters different colours.)
- Mail to the detectives.

Mystery Cupcakes

- Make cupcake mixture from a mix or a favourite recipe.
- Place a lolly inside each cupcake, then bake according to recipe instructions.
- Decorate, then top with gummy footprints.
- Tell the kids to eat carefully and search for a mystery surprise inside!

Prizes and Party Bags

- Mini flashlights
- Magnifying glasses
- Mystery books for young adults
- Detective kits

Costumes

- Ask guests to come dressed as their favourite detectives.

Decorations

- Dim the lights for a spooky atmosphere.
- Add cobwebs (available at costume shops and party shops—or you can make your own by pulling apart cotton wool).
- Provide detective props like torches, magnifying glasses, fingerprint identification kits, notepads and pencils, secret codes, sunglasses, fake noses and so on.
- Tape keys to the walls.
- Set out young adult mysteries.

Games

106 Stage a jewellery store robbery, using props such as costume jewellery, price tags and a shop sign. On slips of paper, write various roles appropriate to your staging, such as jewellers, customers, security guard and so on. Have a non-guest play the robber dressed in dark clothes, hat and mask. Keep the robber out of sight until you give the pre-arranged signal. Have the players act out their roles in the jewellery shop: buying and selling jewellery, polishing the displays, keeping an eye on the customers and so on. After a few minutes, signal the robber to enter the room and cause a commotion, such as knocking over a chair, grabbing some jewels, dropping something, saying something, then fleeing the scene— all in a matter of seconds. After the robbery, have the eyewitnesses get out their notepads. Ask them questions about what they saw during the robbery, such as 'What was the robber wearing', 'What time exactly did the robbery occur', 'What piece of jewellery was stolen', 'What did the robber knock over', 'What did the robber drop', 'What did the robber do first', 'What did the robber say exactly'. After the eyewitnesses write their answers, read them and see how many answers they got right. Award a prize to the eyewitness with the most correct answers.

107 While the detectives sleep, steal items from the room or from the detectives and hide them in another room. When the detectives discover the thefts, announce in what room the items are hidden and have everyone try to find them!

108 Provide an eye mask for each guest. Set out decorative materials, such as ribbons, feathers, beads, glitter, fabric, paper and so on. Let each guest decorate their mask and model it when finished. Take Polaroid snapshots and have the detectives identify the faces behind the masks.

109 Have the detectives make up codes or provide them with codes, such as Morse code, pig Latin or others. Have them relay messages to each other using the codes.

Ages 8–12

Secret Agent Party

Go undercover for this top-secret party.
The event is full of surprises, as the secret
agents try to figure out what's going on!
Put on your trench coats and pull down your
hats—you don't want anyone to see you
having this much fun!

Invitations

- Write the invitation in code and send it to the spy
  recruits. Send the decoder the next day—give the
  spies a day to decode the invitations on their own.
  After the code is broken have the guests call and give
  a coded RSVP.

- If you don't hear from one or two guests send them
  a note telling them how to solve the mysterious
  message.

Secret Code Cake

- Bake a rectangular cake; cool.
- Decorate the cake with chocolate or white icing.
- Write a message in code on top of the cake in a
  contrasting colour of icing.

- Hide the cake so the spies have to find the dessert before they can solve the puzzle on top. Give them clues to the code.

Prizes and Party Bags

- Send the kids home with spy kits, magnifying glasses and plastic glasses with nose disguises.

Costumes

- Have the kids come dressed as their favourite spies, such as James Bond, Inspector Gadget, Harriet the Spy and others.
- When the guests arrive, present them with spy kits—a notepad, a magnifying glass, a pair of plastic glasses and nose, and a code book to use throughout the party.
- Give each kid a code name and a fake passport.

Decorations

- Drape the room in sheets to create secret hiding places for the spies.
- Have the kids give a password at the door. Reveal the password, along with a secret handshake, in the invitation.
- Talk in low voices.

Helful Hint
- Buy a few old trench coats at a second-hand shop in case some of the kids don't have spy costumes.

- Play James Bond music in the background.
- Place cut-out question marks around the room to hide clues for a later game.

Games

110 Play Eye Witness. Have an outsider run into the room, complete a fake crime and escape. Ask the guests questions about what happened and see how many good eye witnesses you have in the group.

111 Have a Mystery Hunt. Hide spy items in the party room, such as a set of fingerprints, a photograph of a suspect, a mysterious message and so on. Announce or stage a crime and tell the kids to collect the evidence. When they have collected all the evidence have them figure out the solution to the crime.

112 Play Bomb Squad. Hide a ticking kitchen timer somewhere in the room and have the kids try to find it before it 'goes off'.

113 Have the spies make their own spy kits. Include powder for making fingerprints, disposable cameras, magnifying glasses, decoders and some puzzles, such as a box with a secret compartment.

114 Divide the kids into two teams and have each team create a puzzle for the other team to solve. Have the puzzles include treasure hunts.

115

Have a mystery meal with one 'poison' item for the kids to detect. Serve lots of little sandwiches with a variety of fillings and spread one with a distinct flavouring, such as curry, garlic or other spice. Hand out the sandwiches and see if the spies can tell which sandwich has been 'poisoned'.

Ages 8–12

Mystery Mayhem

There's no mystery to putting on a Mystery Mayhem party. All you need is a vivid imagination and a few clues on how to make it all happen. So get out your magnifying glasses—it's mystery solving time!

Invitations

- Write out the party invitation on a sheet of paper and make copies for all the party guests. Then cut each copy into puzzle pieces, place in an envelope and mail.

- Write the party details on sheets of paper using an invisible felt-tip pen kit or white crayon. Mail the papers to the guests along with the decoder pen or a dark crayon needed to reveal the invisible message.

- Send clues about the party to the guests each day, offering a little more information each time, until they can finally solve the party details mystery.

Surprise Inside Cake

- Bake a cake and allow it to cool.
- Wrap small toys in plastic bags.

- Scoop out small holes in the cake and insert the toys.
- Turn the cake over and cover it with white icing.
- Make a question mark on top with chocolate icing.
- Slice and serve to kids, making sure to warn them that there are surprises inside.

Prizes and Party Bags

- Send the kids home with magnifying glasses and mystery games.
- Give the guests mystery lollies—small chocolate bars with the outside wrapper removed—to take home and eat.

Costumes

- Ask the kids to wear detective outfits.

- Have the kids come as 'mystery guests'. Let the kids try to guess who everyone is supposed to be.

Variation
- Have a magician come to the party and dazzle the kids with tricks.

Helpful Hint
- Don't make the clues too hard or the games won't be much fun.

Decorations

- Cut out giant question marks from black paper and hang them on the fences, walls and trees.

- Write out curious questions on paper and place them on the table as place mats. You might also ask silly riddles, such as 'Who's buried in Grant's tomb'.

Games

116 Mysterious Footprints: As the guests arrive, make outlines of their shoes or footprints. When you have outlines of all the kids' feet, cut out the prints and mix them up. Have the kids race to find their 'feet'. Then have them try to identify whose feet are whose.

117 Mystery Clue Hunt: Write out a treasure hunt using mysterious clues that lead the players from place to place. Hide the clues all over the yard and send them off in teams to find their way to the treasure.

118 Mystery Map: Draw a map of the yard or park and photocopy it. Mark a path on the map for the kids to follow, looping around and around and finally leading to a mysterious treasure. Make it fun with silly landmarks, such as 'Buzzard Perch' (a tree) and 'Blue Lagoon' (a swimming pool). Divide the kids into teams and see who can find the treasure first.

119 Mystery Message: Divide the players into two teams, with one team in the front yard and the other in the back yard. Have them write mystery riddles about places in the yard, such as 'You'll find a special delivery here' (the letter box) or 'This is where you go if you're bad' (the dog house). Hide treasures at those spots. Exchange messages and yards, and have the teams try to figure out where each other's treasures are hidden.

120 Mystery Star: Give each player a picture of a movie star and a black felt-tip pen. Have them disguise the person with a moustache, warts, hair etc., without letting anyone see. Then hold the pictures up one at a time and see if anyone can recognise the star behind the disguise.

121 Scary Scavenger Hunt: Collect a bunch of silly or disgusting items and hide them around the yard. You might include such things as an empty can of cat food, a rubber snake, plastic vomit, gummy worms and so on. Give the kids a list of the hidden items and see who can find the most.

122 Give the kids inexpensive masks and let them decorate them with puff paints, sequins, feathers, glitter and so on. When the masks are finished, have the kids put them on and try to guess who's behind the mask.

Ages 8–14

Ghosts and Goblins Party

Give the kids a chill thrill with a Ghosts and Goblins Party! Turn the garage into a haunted house or the backyard into a scary cemetery, and make the party frightening, festive and fun!

Invitations

- Make masks from stiff cardboard, cut to fit a child's face. Decorate the masks with puff paints, sequins, feathers and stickers to turn them into whatever you like—Frankenstein, Wolfman, Jason or Freddy, for example. Write the party details on the backs of masks. Attach an elastic string through holes on either side of each mask. Send the masks to guests for an inviting scare. Have the kids wear their masks to the party.

- For added fun, fill the invitation envelopes with a few plastic bugs, ants, or gummy worms.

- If you prefer, send the kids blank masks and ask them to decorate them and wear them to the party.

Graveyard Cake

- Bake a chocolate cake; cool.
- Top with softened chocolate ice cream.
- Crush chocolate wafer cookies to look like finely ground dirt and sprinkle over ice cream.
- Stick lolly snakes into the cake, half-in and half-out.
- Stick oval cookies into the cake to make gravestones. Write funny names on the 'graves' with piping bags.
- Refreeze before serving so the ice cream doesn't melt.

Prizes and Party Bags

- Send the kids home with lolly snakes or other edible critters, or give them plastic bugs and rubber snakes.
- Give the kids monster makeup kits, wax lips and teeth and masks.
- Give the kids scary books about monsters.

Costumes

- Ask the kids to come dressed as a favourite monster, creepy creature or bad guy.
- Award prizes for all kinds of costume categories, such as Scariest, Funniest, Hardest to Make, Hardest to Wear, Most Creative, Most Authentic, Most Disgusting and so on.
- When the kids arrive, provide them with sheets of coloured crepe paper, tape, string and a stapler, and let them design their own costumes.

Decorations

- Create a haunted house in the garage or party room. Cover the windows with black paper and set up scary stations. Have the kids weave through the haunted house one at a time.

Helpful Hint
- If any kids are really scared, let them in on all your secrets so they know it's all in fun.

- Set up a Mad Scientist Laboratory. Have someone dress as a Frankenstein monster and lie on a table among bubbling concoctions (use dry ice and coloured water in clear bowls). Add kitchen utensils, such as tongs, basters and a garlic press, to serve as bizarre scientific instruments.

- Make a Dead Body Storehouse. Dress friends as accident victims, with torn clothes and fake blood and scars. Have them lie on the floor and come to life from time to time, by sitting up, grabbing a passing foot or screaming.

- Create a Pet Cemetery where mangy wild animals look for food. Have someone dress as a dog, a bear or other animal and give them large soup bones to hold. Have them make wild growling noises and threatening gestures as kids pass by.

- Make a Witches Cauldron. Dress the witches in long, grey wigs and black dresses, colour their fingernails black, black out a tooth or two and have them stir a cauldron with a broom. Inside the cauldron place wet noodles or jelly.

Games

123 Play Body Pieces. Have the kids sit in a circle in a dimly lit room while you make up a story about a mean old witch who falls apart, piece by piece. As you talk about each body part, pass around a paper bag lined with a plastic bag and have the kids feel inside without looking. The bag should contain the 'body part' that fell off, such as peeled grapes for eyeballs, a canned apricot for a tongue, popcorn kernels for teeth, cooked spaghetti for brains, a large peeled tomato for a heart, cooked macaroni noodles for intestines, a slab of jelly for the liver and so on. Have the kids guess what you used for the body parts, then reveal the foods.

124 Create your own monsters using cardboard boxes or old clothing. Divide the kids into teams of three or four players. Give each team a variety of arts and crafts materials, along with boxes and clothes, and have them create monsters using their imaginations. Display the monsters at the end of activity time and award prizes to each team.

125 Make a Creepy Crawly Critter Collection. Place a bag of plastic or candy bugs and worms into a large bowl, mix with jelly and wet noodles, and have the kids dig through in the bowl to find the critters.

126 Turn the kids into monsters. Create a tunnel out of large cardboard boxes, making windows along the way. Have the kids climb through the tunnel and, as they come to a window, apply fake blood and scars, masks and so on. The kids come out of the tunnel looking like monsters!

Inquiring Snoop Party

What's the scoop? An Inquiring Snoop Party! Let the guests read all about it in a special edition invitation! Then give the mild-mannered reporters a peek into the fast-paced newspaper world!

Invitations

- Create a mock-up invitation using a real newspaper front page. First, type the party details, formatted to look like a special news column. Cut and paste your column between a couple of real newspaper stories. Then photocopy the entire page, making enough for all your guests. Mail the invitations or, if possible, insert your paper into your guests' morning newspapers.

- Create your own personal newsletter using desktop publishing software; add pictures, headlines and other details.

Daily News Cake

- Bake a cake; cool.
- Decorate the cake with white icing.

- For a birthday cake, write a Happy Birthday headline across the top.
- Draw columns on the cake using chocolate icing and a fine-point tube.
- Fill the columns with horizontal lines to simulate type.
- Add smaller headlines to complete the page.

Prizes and Party Bags

- Send the kids home with copies of the newspaper front pages from the days they were born. Obtain newspapers from library files.
- Give each kid a book featuring a popular newspaper comic strip.

Costumes

- Have the kids come dressed as newspaper people— reporters, photographers, gossip columnists, movie reviewers, obituary writers, even managing editors.
- Suggest that the kids find their costumes at a local second-hand shop, where they're sure to have trench coats, hats and other newspaper-related accessories.

Decorations

- Hang newspapers on the walls to create the feeling of a newsroom. Spread newspapers over the table as a tablecloth.

- Make paper hats from newspapers for the kids to wear.
- Create phony headlines about the guests and post them around the room.
- Search the libraries for copies of newspapers from the guests' birthdays and use them as place mats. Give them as presents to take home.

Variation

- Arrange to visit a newspaper office and get a tour of the place. Let the kids see real reporters, photographers, printer, and editors at work.

Helpful Hint

- Newspaper ink rubs off easily on the hands, so keep some wet wipes nearby to clean up the mess.

Games

127 Play Headlines. At the library, search through newspapers or news magazines and write down events that happened over the past year. Form questions using the information you've accumulated and have the kids guess in what month each event took place.

128 Play Headlines with news photos instead of headlines.

129 Instead of having the kids guess the month, make the game easier by having them place the events in order.

130 Have a Word Search. Give each player a sheet of newspaper. Call out a word. Whoever finds that word first on the paper wins a prize.

131 Play the Comic Strip Game. Cut out one colour comic strip for each guest from the Sunday paper. Cut the strips into individual squares and place them in envelopes. Distribute the envelopes to guests and see if they can put the strips together in the correct order. Once everyone finishes, exchange the envelopes and play again.

132 Vary the Comic Strip Game. Mix all the squares together and have the kids try to pick out the comic strips that go together—in the correct order!

133 Have the kids create their own newspaper using paper, felt-tip pens and photographs cut out from magazines.

134 Fold newspapers into hats or boats, using instructions from library books that feature paper folding.

135 Have the kids cut up headlines and combine them to make silly new headlines. For example, the headlines 'Dead Skunk Found in Park' and 'Cold Weather Expected Today' could become 'Dead Skunk Expected Today'.

136 Let the kids draw their own comic strips.

Ages 8–16

It's a Mystery Party

You never know what's going to happen when you host a mystery party because—it's a mystery! Play detective, set the clues, and keep the guests guessing with lots of surprises, puzzles and crimes to solve.

Invitations

- Send puzzling invitations for the kids to solve. For example, write the invitations in your own creative code. The next day send the key to the code; that way the guests will have to wonder for a little while what the invitations say before they can read them!

- Give the kids clues to find the party invitations. Don't tell them what they're looking for, only that it's hidden somewhere on their property.

- Write the party invitations, cut them into puzzle pieces, and mail the pieces in envelopes to your guests.

- Mail the pieces of the invitation puzzles one at a time, instead of all at once!

Mystery Cake

- Bake a cake; cool.
- Slice the cake into individual pieces, one piece for each guest. Be sure to keep the slices together.
- Scoop out a tiny amount of cake from each slice.
- Fill the holes with small toys and carefully turn the cake over.
- Cover the cake with icing. Decorate it with question marks made with a piping bag.
- Serve the pre-cut slices and warn the kids there's a surprise inside each slice!

Prizes and Party Bags

- Hand out mystery puzzles.
- Give the kids Mystery Candy. Unwrap chocolate bars and cover them with foil—for the kids to guess what the chocolate bar is.

Costumes

- Have the guests dress as detectives, crime solvers, police officers or spies.
- When the kids arrive, give them disguises, such as wigs, hats, glasses, moles and so on. Then have them create new identities to go with their costumes.

Decorations

- Make the party room dark, spooky, and mysterious. Decorate the walls with masks, costume pieces and cobwebs; cover the walls and windows with black paper and dim the lights.

Variation

- Ask a police officer or detective visit the party to talk about police work.

Helpful Hint

- Don't make the puzzles too difficult, or they won't be fun to solve. Keep them simple and give lots of clues!

- Set up a cave by draping blankets and sheets over the furniture. Then have the party 'underground'.

Games

137 Have a Mystery Crime Hunt. Divide the kids into teams, and have a scavenger hunt for mysterious items you've set out ahead of time in the party room or the yard. When the kids collect all the items, have them figure out what crime goes with the 'evidence'. For example, for a jewellery robbery, have the kids find a necklace, a mask, fingerprints, a screwdriver, a getaway bag and a false moustache.

138 Play Decipher. Divide players into teams, give each team paper and a pencil and tell them to design codes for the other team. Have them solve the codes.

139 Play Touch-and-Tell. Wrap a number of small items. Have the kids sit in a circle. Pass the items from player to player, and have them guess the item. The player who guesses correctly keeps the item and drops out of the game.

140 Have the kids make code books using Morse code, sign language or other methods of communication. Then have the kids relay messages back and forth, singly or in teams.

141 Before the party begins, record noises from everyday life. During the party, play the recording, and have the kids guess the mystery sounds.

142 Serve Mystery Soup. Have each guest bring a can of soup with the label removed. Combine all the soups in a large pot, heat and serve.

143 Blindfold the kids before serving snacks; then have them guess what they are eating.

144 Have a surprise Popcorn Explosion. Spread out a sheet and have the kids sit around the edges. Place a popcorn maker in the centre and prepare popcorn according to package directions— but DO NOT cover the popcorn maker. Let the kids watch the popcorn pop onto the sheet. Make sure everyone stays away from the popper while it's on so they don't get sprayed with hot oil or kernels. Let the kids gobble up the popcorn when the popping is done.

Ages 10–14

Secret Séance

A Secret Séance party is the perfect way to find out what the future may bring!

Invitation

- For each guest, fold a sheet of white paper in half.
- Draw a circle, leaving off a 5 centimetre segment where the fold is.
- Cut out the circle, leaving the fold uncut; this makes a round card that opens at the top.
- On the outside of the card, write 'Come and Find Out Your Future . . .'
- Write the party details inside the card; mail.

Tarot cards

- Buy or make tarot cards, three cards for each guest.
- Write party details on the cards using fortune-telling phrases, such as 'I see lots of fun in your future at the Secret Séance party on Friday night'.
- Tuck the cards in an envelope and mail.

Chocolate Spiders

- Bake a cake; cool.
- Melt 1 cup of chocolate chips in a saucepan over low heat.
- Mix in 1 cup of crispy rice cereal and 1 cup of shredded coconut.
- Drop spoonfuls of the chocolate mixture onto wax paper to make spider bodies.
- In a separate saucepan, melt 1 cup of chocolate chips.
- Stir in 1 cup of chow mein noodles; let cool.
- Carefully pick out chocolate-covered noodles and stick to bodies to make legs.
- Add dots of orange icing for eyes.
- Put spiders on top of cake and serve.

Prizes and Party Bags

- Ghost Pops: Cover lollipops with white tissues, secure with black ribbon, dot eyes on with black felt-tip pen.
- Glow-in-the-dark T-shirts
- Tarot cards
- Magic tricks

Costumes

- Have guests wear gypsy costumes and have them bring fortune-telling games, tarot cards and so on.

Decorations

- Hang streamers from the centre of the ceiling to each wall, letting the streamers hang down the walls.
- Use coloured light bulbs in lamps.
- Place a table in the centre of the room and cover with a red, black, or decorated tablecloth.
- Place a chair for each guest at the table. Make place markers from tarot cards.
- Set a crystal ball (available at toy and magic shops) in the middle of the table. Or make one by setting a small fishbowl upside down on a plate.

- Using glow-in-the-dark paper, cut out eyes, skeletons and faces and tape them to the walls, drapes, ceiling and séance table.

- Draw outlines of your hand, cut them out and draw lines on them for detail. Tape them to the walls or to the table.

- Play spooky music.

Games

145 Divide the guests into two teams and place each team in a separate room. Have each team make up silly fortunes for the other team, such as 'You will marry Prince William', 'You will become a famous rapper', or 'You will live on a houseboat'. Have them write the fortunes on slips of paper, roll the slips, insert them into balloons, inflate the balloons and tie them off. Regroup and have one team place its balloons on one side of the room and the other team place its balloons on the opposite side. Have members of each team take turns choosing a balloon from the other team's side, popping the balloon and reading the fortune inside.

146 Choose one player to be the Mind Reader. Ask the Mind Reader to leave the room and secretly give them a note that reads 'After I point to something blue, the next item will be the selected item'. Have a player select an item in the room, then ask the Mind Reader to return. Tell the group the Mind Reader will identify the selected item when you point to it. As you point to non-blue items, the Mind Reader should shake their head. Then point to a blue item, which will alert the Mind Reader that the next item is the selected item. Point to the selected item. The Mind Reader should nod and exclaim, 'That's it!' to the amazement of the group. Keep playing until someone figures out the trick.

147 Have everyone sit at the séance table and join hands. Turn off the lights. Have surprise guests stand behind a curtain or doorway and hint who they are in weird voices. You might include an older sister, a friend who's moved away, a grandparent, a teacher, a scout leader, one of the guest's parents and so on. After each surprise guest has spoken to the group, turn on the lights and reveal his or her identity.

148 Hide a number of scary items around the room, such as a rubber hand, plastic eyeball, ball of slime, toy snake and so on. Turn off the lights and have the kids try to find the scary items in the dark!

149 Have everyone sit at the séance table. Ask each guest to tell a ghost story. Or have the guests join hands and ask one guest to begin a ghost story. After a few sentences, the storyteller stops and squeezes the hand of the guest on their left. That guest must continue with the story. Let everyone have a turn adding to the story. The guest who started the story concludes it.

Variation: Have the storyteller hold a torch under their chin while telling the story. When it's time to move to the next guest, the storyteller shines the light on someone else's face, who must then take the torch and continue the story.

150 Provide white makeup and face paints and have guests design scary faces on one another. Award a prize to the designer of the scariest face!

151 Buy a dark T-shirt for each guest (or ask each to bring one). Buy glow-in-the-dark paints and markers. Let the guests draw monster faces, skeletons or other scary designs on the T-shirts. Then have them put on the T-shirts, turn out the lights and watch the spooky images glow.

152 Message-from-Beyond Sandwich: Write messages on bread slices using a toothpick and milk. Have guests toast their bread first and read the mysterious messages on the slices.

Food Parties

Whether the kids love making
or tasting yummy dishes, this collection
of games will bring out some culinary
creativity!

Ages 4–10

Batty Biscuit Party

Everyone loves biscuits, so why not have
a party that offers biscuits from start to
finish?! Invite the cookie monsters to the
party and watch the kooky fun begin!

Invitations

- Bake one-of-a-kind biscuit invitations that will
  delight your guests. Mix a favourite recipe of hearty
  biscuits—sugar, gingerbread, or peanut butter work
  best. Cut dough into large circles or biscuit cutter
  shapes and bake according to directions. Remove
  from oven and insert icy-pole sticks into warm
  biscuits to make biscuit pops. Cool, then decorate
  with a piping bag, adding the party details on the
  biscuits and the icy-pole stick. Tie a ribbon around
  the stick, place the biscuit pops in small boxes with
  tissue paper, and hand deliver to guests.

Giant Biscuit Cake

- Bake two round chocolate cakes; cool.
- Cover the sides of one layer with chocolate icing.
- Decorate the sides with chocolate sprinkles.
- Cover the top of the iced layer with white icing, marshmallow cream or vanilla ice cream, about 12 millimetres thick.
- Place the second round chocolate cake on top of the first layer.
- Cover the top layer with chocolate icing and decorate with chocolate sprinkles.

Prizes and Party Bags

- Send the kids home with a box of store-bought biscuits, a bag of homemade biscuits, or a collection of biscuits from your biscuit exchange.
- Give each guest a biscuit book and some biscuit cutters.

Costumes

- Have the kids be creative and dress as favourite biscuits.
- Have the kids use biscuits to decorate hats to wear to the party.

Helpful Hints
- Offer lots of food alternatives so the kids don't get overloaded on sweets.
- Use biscuit cutters to give alternate foods interesting shapes.

- Make biscuit costumes when the guests arrive. Use large sheets of poster board, paper and felt-tip pens. Cut out large circles, rectangles or other shapes from the poster board, depending on the shape of the biscuit you want to create, such as Tim Tams, wafer biscuits, or cheese biscuits. Cover the poster board with paper or colour with felt-tip pens. Make two matching shapes for each guest, and attach them at the shoulders with string or ribbon.

Decorations

- Cut out pictures of biscuits from magazines or old cook books and glue them onto paper. Use the posters to decorate the party room. Hang biscuit cut-outs from the ceiling or tape them to the walls of the party room.

- Decorate the tablecloth with drawings, cut-outs or real biscuits.

- Set out biscuit cookbooks for added decoration.

- Make a giant biscuit to greet the guests at the door. Cut out a large circle from brown poster board and decorate it with real biscuits.

Games

153 Have a Cookie Contest! Buy a variety of biscuits and break them into small bites, so there is one piece of each type for each guest. Place each broken up variety into a separate paper bag. Pass the bags around one at a time, and have the kids take a taste without looking. Have the kids write down their guesses, and see who can name the most biscuits.

154 Try a Biscuit-Bite-Off. Have one player taste a piece of biscuit. If that player can identify the cookie type, he or she goes on to taste the next biscuit. If the player cannot name the biscuit, that player drops out of line and the next player continues. Play until only one player remains.

155 Have the kids invent their own new biscuit, using ingredients from popular biscuit recipes, such as peanut butter, chocolate chips, sprinkles, nuts and so on. Divide the kids into groups and have a taste test at the end of the biscuit creation to see which recipe tastes best.

156 Have the cooks shape the biscuits into large monster faces, decorated with icing and sprinkles. Whoever has the funniest, scariest or strangest monster biscuit wins a prize.

157 Host a biscuit exchange. Ask the kids to bring two to three dozen favourite homemade biscuits. Place the biscuit collections on the table, count them to figure out how many biscuits each kid can take, and let the kids take that number of biscuits from each pile to take home.

Ages 5–8

Lolly and Cake Party

Kids love sugar and spice and everything nice, so invite them to a smile-makin' Lolly and Cake Party, featuring all their favourite treats.

Invitations

- Buy a bunch of chocolate bars and carefully remove all the wrappers. Set the chocolate bars aside. Write the party details inside the wrappers using a permanent felt-tip pen, or insert a separate piece of paper with the party information inside the wrapper. Fold the wrappers back up without the chocolate and place them in envelopes to mail to the kids. Save the chocolate bars for a game.

- If you prefer, send the chocolate bar, too. Write the party details inside the wrappers, then tape them back together around the chocolate bars and mail them in padded envelopes.

Box of Lollies Cake

- Make chocolate and/or vanilla cupcakes; cool.
- Decorate with chocolate icing.

- Decorated with tiny lollies.
- Set the cupcakes in a big dress box lined with foil.
- Close the box lid and cover the entire box with velvet wrapping to look like a giant box of lollies, complete with bow.
- Open the box and serve the giant cupcake bonbons.

Helpful Hints
- To make sure the kids don't overeat the sweet stuff, offer them lolly bags to store the goodies for later.
- Make regular 'lolly snack' times when each kid is allowed to eat one treat. Signal snack times with a bell or a whistle.

Prizes and Party Bags

- Send the kids home with a handful of chocolate gold coins.
- Give the kids mysterious chocolate bars wrapped only in foil so they have to guess what kind of chocolate bar it is.
- Offer each guest his or her own personal small box of chocolates.
- Treat the kids to giant lollipops.

Costumes

- Have the kids dress up as lollies or use lollies as accessories to decorate some sweet-looking costumes. Tell the kids there will be an award for best lolly costume, so they should be creative!

Decorations

- Set out colourful lollies everywhere in the party room—all sizes, shapes and kinds.
- Using old cook books or magazines, cut out pictures of goodies and make a collage to hang on the wall or to place on the tablecloth.
- Write the kids' names on chocolate bars and set the chocolate bars on the table as place markers.
- Spell out the kids' names at each place setting using chocolate chips.
- Decorate the front door with lollies to greet your guests. Glue paper-wrapped lollies to large sheets of poster board. Cover the front door with the lolly-covered poster board. Watch the delighted faces arrive at your door.

Games

158 Have a Chocolate Bar Taste Test. Unwrap some chocolate bars, break them into bits in separate bowls and let the kids taste each one. Then have them try to guess the chocolate bar names.

159 Unwrap the chocolate bars and rewrap them in foil. Then let the kids guess the brands just by looking at the shapes.

160 Play the Chocolate Catch Game. Have the kids sit in a circle. Place a bunch of chocolate bars (one for each player) in the centre of the circle. Give each player four playing cards and place the remainder of the deck in the middle. One player begins by drawing a new card from the deck and passing a card to the player on the left. The next player passes a card to the left and so on to the end, where a card is discarded. Each player tries to collect four of one suit. When a player has four of one suit, he or she quietly takes a chocolate bar from the centre, while continuing to pass cards. When others notice someone has taken a chocolate bar, they are to follow suit, grabbing up a chocolate bar as quickly as possible. The last one to take a chocolate bar is out, but gets to keep the chocolate as a consolation prize. Replenish the supply and continue playing until only one player remains.

161 Make Lifesaver necklaces. Have the kids string the lollies on thread or thin shoelace licorice. The kids can then wear the necklaces for the rest of the party.

Ages 7–10

Party Picnic

Have a portable Party Picnic and take your fun and games with you. You can set up the picnic in the backyard, or take it to the park or playground and spend the day enjoying food and fun.

Invitations

- Send the kids the party details written on paper picnic napkins.
- Fold up tiny tablecloths with the party information written inside and mail to guests.
- Cut out giant ants from black paper, write the party details in white ink, and mail to the guests.
- Fold brown paper into cards and decorate them with felt-tip pen to look like wicker baskets. Write the party details inside and mail to guests.
- Enclose plastic ants in the envelope for an extra surprise.

Dirt and Worms Cupcakes

- Bake chocolate cupcakes and decorate with chocolate icing.
- Cover with chocolate biscuit crumbs or chocolate sprinkles.
- Stick a lolly snake into the top of the cupcake. Let half the snake hang out over the side.
- Stick a plastic flower in the centre and serve to the kids.

Prizes and Party Bags

- Give the kids a collection of plastic bugs to take home.
- Give out butterfly nets.

- Give the guests mini picnic baskets for their own picnics.
- Send the kids home with their own frisbees.

Helpful Hint

- Check to see if any of the kids have outdoor or food allergies before the picnic.

Costumes

- Have the kids wear shorts and tops if the weather is warm, tracksuits and athletic gear if it's cool.

Decorations

- Find a large check tablecloth for your party and lay it on the table or on the ground for the picnic.
- Set colourful paper plates at each place setting. Write the guests' names around the rims of the plates.
- Set a picnic basket filled with fruit, cheese and biscuits in the centre of the tablecloth.
- Cut out ants from black paper or buy plastic ants from the toy shop. Place the ants all around the picnic area.

Games

162 Pie-Eating Contest: Set a bunch of mini pies on the picnic table, making sure you have one for each player. On the word 'Go' have the kids race to eat their pies without using their hands. The first one to finish a pie wins a prize. You can also have a drinking contest by filling small bowls with punch and having the contestants lap them up without using their hands.

163 Seed Spit: Set out bowls one metre away from each contestant. Have players sit down with a slice of watermelon, eat the melon and try to spit the seeds into the bowls. The player with the most seeds in the bowl wins the game.

164 Give the kids small picnic baskets and let them colour the baskets with paints, felt-tip pens or puff paints. Let the kids take the baskets home when they are dry for their own little picnics.

165 After the big picnic meal, have everyone lie on their backs on the tablecloth and stare at the clouds. Tell the kids to describe what they see in the clouds. See who can find the weirdest and funniest shapes in the clouds.

Ages 7–12

Now You're Cookin'

At this party, you'll be cookin' all night, making and eating snacks!

Biscuit Pop

- Roll out refrigerated biscuit dough and cut out large circles by pressing a drinking glass upside down into the dough.
- Bake according to packet directions.
- While the biscuits bake, write party details on icy-pole stocks, one for each guest.
- Remove the biscuits from oven and immediately insert an icy-pole stick into the side of each biscuit to make a biscuit pop; let biscuits harden.
- Using icing, write 'Now You're Cookin'' or draw a funny face on each biscuit.
- Tie each biscuit pop with ribbon and hand deliver.

Slumber Party Recipe

- Buy recipe cards or make your own by using coloured index cards.
- For each guest, write the following recipe for a fun slumber party:
  —Gather ingredients: Friends, pyjamas, sleeping bags and recipes for favourite snacks.

Brownie Pizza Cake

- Make brownie mixture according to packet directions and pour into a pizza pan. Top with lollies, mini marshmallows, nuts and sprinkles; bake, drizzle with caramel sauce and cool.

Prizes and Party Bags

- Fun cooking utensils
- Kids' cookbooks
- Decorated aprons

- Ask each cook to bring a recipe for a favourite snack and the ingredients to make it. Or have each mail their recipe to you ahead of time, and you buy the ingredients.

Decorations

- Host the party in the kitchen and dining room.
- Create an elegant look—fancy tablecloth, china, silverware and candles—or a casual, fun look— funny place mats, silly eating utensils and colourful paper plates.
- Cut out pictures of gourmet food and use them as place mats.
- Use hollowed-out oranges for drinking glasses, hollowed-out watermelon and coconut shells for bowls, tortillas for plates and so on.
- Set out all the utensils and appliances you'll need and tape funny labels to each one, such as 'Milkshake Maker' for the blender and 'Whirligig' for the eggbeater.
- Tape food posters to the walls.
- Hang a row of plain white aprons on the wall, one for each cook to decorate then wear while cooking.

Games

166 Choose a variety of foods with interesting textures, such as cheese spread, salsa, chocolate syrup, buttermilk and creamed corn. Place each food in a separate bowl and cover with foil. Have players pair up and blindfold one player in each pair. Have the other player feed their partner a taste of each food, who in turn must guess the food they tasted. Award a prize to the pair who gets the most correct answers. Have partners switch blindfolds and play again with new foods to taste.

167 Provide a plain white apron for each guest. Let the guests decorate their aprons with fabric pens, markers, puff paints, iron-on transfers and other decorative items. When the aprons are dry, have the guests wear them while cooking.

168

Cut watermelon, cantaloupe, melons and bananas into bite-size pieces and place each fruit in a separate bowl. Set out bowls of strawberries, blueberries, mandarin and orange slices and grapes. Cut the bottom off a head of cabbage and set the cabbage on the table. Using toothpicks, stick two strawberries on the front of the cabbage to make the porcupine's eyes, a grape to make the nose and a mandarin or orange slice to make the mouth. Have the guests stick fruits onto long wooden skewers. When skewers are loaded, stick them into the cabbage to make porcupine quills. After the guests admire their new friend, they can gobble him up!

169 Make pancake batter according to packet directions. Let cooks carefully spoon batter into a frying pan and cook the pancakes until brown on both sides; place on a platter. Provide flavoured syrups, fruit pieces and jams. Let the cooks decorate their pancakes to look like faces. Have the cooks guess who the pancakes look like before eating.

170 Provide a variety of ice cream flavours and large biscuits. Let the kids sandwich a scoop of ice cream between two biscuits. Provide bowls of sprinkles and chocolate chips and let the cooks roll the edges of their sandwiches in the treats.

Ages 8–14

Cooks in the Kitchen Party

What's the recipe for a really great party? Take a handful of invitations, add some decorations, throw in some games and activities, and add a heaped measure of do-it-yourself food. Mix well with a roomful of guests and enjoy your Cooks in the Kitchen Party!

Invitations

- Buy or make blank recipe cards for your guests. Write down the recipe for a special treat on one side and the party details on the other side (phrase the party details to read like a recipe). Then send the recipe card, along with the special treat (the one for which you wrote the recipe), to your guests.

- Send small cooking utensils along with the invitations and ask your guests to bring them back to the party.

Easy-bake Mini Cakes

- Buy a large muffin tin or a set of small round cake pans.

- Bake large muffins or small cakes, one for each guest; cool.

- Give each guest a cake or muffin.

- Set out bowls of variously coloured icing, piping bags, sprinkles and sugar decorations. Give the kids plastic knives.

Variations

- Take the kids to a cooking school and let them see the experts at work.

- Ask a local restaurant for a behind-the-scenes look at the kitchen, then stay for lunch or dinner.

Helpful Hints

- Check with parents to see if any kids have food allergies. Make sure you don't use those foods.

- Have the kids wear aprons—cooking can get messy.

- Keep the recipes quick and easy, and make recipe cards enlarged and illustrated so they are easy to follow.

- Let the kids ice and decorate their individual cakes.

Prizes and Party Bags

- Send the kids home with recipes of the foods you've made at the party, so they can cook the same foods at home.

- Give your guests kids' cookbooks.

- Offer the kids a special food treat.

- Give the kids their own special cooking utensil, such as a turkey baster filled with lollies, a ladle filled with nuts, or an egg whip filled with fairy floss.

Costumes

- Ask the kids to come dressed as chefs or provide large white men's shirts for your guests. You can find inexpensive shirts at second-hand shops.

- Make big fluffy chef's hats out of white or coloured crepe paper. First make a headband from the crepe paper. Cut out a big circle from crepe paper and puff it out in the middle. Wrap the headband around the outside bottom of the pouf, and staple or glue the pouf and the band together. Place the hats on the chefs' heads as they arrive.

Decorations

- Decorate the party room to look like a special restaurant. Include menus, a fancy tablecloth, your best silverware and other special touches.
- Decorate the kitchen with lots of cooking supplies tied with ribbons.
- Put up pictures of food, set out a variety of cookbooks and group ingredients together for a game to be played later.

Games

171 Set collections of ingredients together, one collection for several teams of two to three kids. For example, you may have pizza ingredients on the counter, biscuit ingredients near the stove and cake supplies by the sink. Have the kids move from station to station, and try to guess what the ingredients will make.

172 Play the Food-Tasting Game. Blindfold the kids; serve them a food you have cooked before the party and have them guess what the food is. Then reveal the treat.

173 Play Name That Ingredient. Have the kids taste a new food and guess the ingredients. Put something unusual in your recipe to make guessing a challenge, such as a banana in peanut butter biscuits.

174 Eat what you cook! Make mini-pizzas from English muffins, macaroni and cheese with unusual noodles, do-it-yourself tacos, peanut butter chocolate chip biscuits, two-flavour ice-cream pie, confetti pasta salad with colourful cut-up vegetables.

Ages 8–15

Restaurant/ Café Party

Open your own restaurant for the day and invite hungry patrons to come and dine in your one-of-a-kind eatery. With a little imagination you can turn your dining room into a diner, your kitchen into a café, or your party room into a pizza parlor. What's on the menu? Fun!

Invitations

- Make homemade menus. Instead of food items, write the party details inside.

- If your party has a diner theme, copy a diner menu and add party details under the food listings.

- If your party theme is a French café, add a few French words to the party details.

- If your party theme is a high-school cafeteria, print your menu on the back of a school notice.

- If you prefer, write your party details on fancy or cartoon napkins; mail to guests.

Menu Cake

- Bake a cake; cool.
- Decorate the cake with white icing.
- Write the name of your restaurant at the top of the cake, and add menu selections with piping bags.

Helful Hint
- Be sure to check with parents regarding food allergies so all the kids can enjoy the party without problems.

- Name the restaurant and each of the food selections after one of the guests, such as Sammy's Sherbet or Zack's Zucchini Squares.

Prizes and Party Bags

- Send the kids home with rolls of refrigerated biscuit dough so they can make dessert themselves.
- Give the guests recipes for special treats along with nicely packaged appropriate ingredients.

Costumes

- Have your guests dress in a style appropriate to your restaurant theme:
  — For a '50s diner, have the kids dress in '50s style, with jeans and leather jackets or poodle skirts and cardigan sweaters.
  — For a French café, have the kids dress in their best clothes.

— For a high-school cafeteria, the kids should dress like teenagers.

Decorations

- Pick your favourite restaurant style and decorate the room accordingly:
  — For a '50s diner, decorate with lots of records, old photos and play old rock and roll tunes.
  — For a French café, put up French posters and flags and play French music.
  — For a high-school cafeteria, decorate the room in school colours and put up banners and pennants.

Games

175 Give the kids a collection of entrée ingredients, and ask them to make creatures using the provided ingredients. They can work in small groups or individually. Include such food items as a variety of crackers, cut-up vegetables and fruit, nuts and seeds, and bonding items, such as cream cheese, peanut butter and other spreads. Award prizes for such categories as Scariest, Funniest and so on.

176 Offer entrées from different countries and have the kids guess the ingredients—and the country of origin.

177

Divide the kids into small groups and have each group create a new food with ingredients you provided. For example, you may give one group the ingredients for chocolate chip biscuits, but add several optional ingredients, such as seeds, dried fruit, coconut and so on, so the kids can be creative. After the groups create their food masterpieces, let them name their treats. Then have a taste test to determine which creation tastes yummiest, strangest, most creative and so on.

World Traveller Parties

These exciting parties will take the party-goers to another place altogether!

Ages 2–10

Locomotion Party

Since kids are always on the go, why not provide them with a way to get there—a Locomotion Party! Hop on board and take a trip to party land. You never know where you'll end up!

Invitations

- Create giant tickets inviting your guests to the Locomotion Party. Copy a plane or train ticket, or make up your own using paper and felt-tip pens or a computer and printer. Make the destination the party house and include arrival and departure times.

- Send the kids postcards with 'Wish you were here!' written on the front and the party details written on the back.

- Tuck the invitations inside travel brochures or format them to read and look like travel brochures.

Train Cake

- Bake or buy one small square cake for each guest.
- Have the kids decorate their cakes to look like train cars, using a variety of icing, decorations and lollies.
- When finished, line the cakes up to make a train.

Prizes and Party Bags

- Give the kids key rings to take home. Attach their initials or a toy plane, train or car.
- Hand out address books so the kids can keep in touch.
- Provide small picture books with a travel theme.
- Give the kids compasses to help them find their way home.

Costumes

- Ask the kids to come dressed as transportation workers, such as railroad engineers, flight attendants, cruise ship directors or bus drivers.

Variations

- Take the party on the road to visit an airport, cruise ship, train or fire station. If you call ahead you can often arrange a behind-the-scenes tour for the kids.
- Go to a car show or race.
- Take the kids to a small-car driving range for fun.

Helpful Hint

- If offering a wide variety of transportation themes seems too much, keep the party simple by focusing on just one type of locomotion.

- Have the kids come dressed as tourists ready to travel the world.

Decorations

- Hang up posters of faraway lands and exotic locations.
- Play music from foreign countries in the background.
- Cut maps into pieces to use as place mats. Use a couple of unfolded maps as a tablecloth.
- Set the scene by creating the interior of a plane, train or boat. For a plane, set up two rows of chairs, use a TV as the in-flight movie screen and serve food on TV trays. Drape a sheet from the ceiling in an arch to form the plane's roof. Do the same for a train, except for the movie screen. For a boat, set up lawn chairs in a row and serve the food buffet-style. Hang fishnets on the walls. Make portholes using paper, with fish on the other side of the 'glass', and hang them on the walls.

Games

178 Play Where in the World? Cut out sections of a map and have the kids try to guess where in the world they belong.

179 Give clues about famous sites around the world and have the kids guess the location.

180 Show postcards or posters from foreign lands and let the kids identify the places.

181 Play Musical Train Seats (or plane or bus). Set up enough chairs for all but one guest. Play music and have the kids walk around the chairs. When you stop the music, the kids scramble for a chair. Whoever does not find a seat is out. Remove one chair and play again. Continue playing until only one player remains.

182 Provide cardboard boxes about the size of a microwave oven so the kids can fit them around their bodies. Have one box for each guest. Decide whether you want to make train cars, automobiles, individual planes or something else in which the kids can travel. Then cut windows, doors, and holes for arms and legs as needed. Let the kids paint the boxes to look like train carriages, cars and so on. Then have the kids 'travel' around outdoors.

Ages 4–12

Pirate Ship Party

Sail off to Pirate's Cove for a hearty party aboard ship. All you need are cardboard boxes and paint to turn your party place into a pirate ship! Yo-ho, yo-ho, it's a Pirate Ship Party for us!

Invitations

- Help your guests find their way to Pirate's Cove with a Treasure Map invitation. Draw a simple map of your neighbourhood, including the homes of each guest and your own. Mark your home with an X, then add familiar sights, and give them creative names, such as Hangman's Tree, Dead Man's Mall and Peg-Leg's Restaurant. Photocopy the map and personalise each map by making a dotted-line path from the guest's house to the party house. Tear or burn the edges, roll the maps into scrolls, secure with gold strings and mail.

- For fun, put the Treasure Map scrolls inside empty plastic bottles to create an Invitation in a Bottle. Hand deliver to guests. Let them figure out how to retrieve the invitations!

- Attach eye patches or plastic swords to the invitations.

Treasure Chest Cake

- Bake a rectangular cake; cool.

- Cover with chocolate icing. Decorate with colourful sprinkles and chocolate gold coins to make it look like a chest lid.

- Clean the baking pan, then frost the outside sides of the pan.

- Set the pan at a right angle to the cake to form a treasure chest.

- Fill the chest with lolly jewellery and chocolate gold coins.

- Send the pirates home with their loot— chocolate gold coins, eye patches, swords, costume parts, flags and fake jewellery.

Helful Hint
- Be sure to keep the homemade swords dull—no sharp points—and supervise the sword fights.

Costumes

- Ask the kids to dress as pirates.

- Buy pirate-wear at a second-hand shop and let the kids dress up at the party.

- Provide eye patches and swords, fake jewellery, handkerchiefs and phony moustaches. Dot the kids' faces with black eye pencil to create 'three-day beards'.

Decorations

- With a little imagination, you can turn the party area into a Pirate's Cove. Get a few large boxes and line them up to form the foundation of your pirate ship. Open the boxes at the top and cut openings between connecting boxes to form sections of the ship. Cut out round windows along the sides. Form a 'walk-the-plank' entrance by cutting an opening on one side of the ship and laying the cardboard piece on the floor. Bend the cardboard boxes into a point at both ends of the ship to form the fore and aft. Paint the whole ship brown, raise a crow's nest using a hat rack or an old lamp post and attach a pirate flag. You're ready to sail!

Games

183 Play Walk the Plank! Set out a two-metre long wooden board. Line the kids up at one end. Beginning with easy challenges, have the kids walk straight across the flat part of the board without stepping off into the 'sea'. After everyone has completed the first task, increase the difficulty level. Have the kids walk the plank backwards, sideways, hopping, without using their hands for balance, with weights on both arms to obscure balance, passing over an obstacle set in the middle, and—for the ultimate challenge—blindfolded! When a pirate falls into the sea, he or she must drop out of the game. When only one pirate remains, award a prize.

184 Have a Treasure Hunt. Hide some chocolate gold coins around the yard or party room, and let the kids hunt for them. Make sure everyone gets a handful of coins when the hunt is over.

185 Make eye patches for the pirates. Cut the eye patches from felt or imitation leather and attach a length of elastic string on both sides.

186 Make swords. Cut out short lengths of cardboard and round the tips. Cut two smaller pieces as the crossbars and glue or staple the crossbars to the swords. Paint the blades silver and the handles black. Let the kids decorate their own swords.

187 Make pirate flags. Give each kid a rectangular piece of lining material or cotton and permanent felt-tip pens. Let them colour their own pirate flags. Staple the finished flags to dowels.

Ages 6–12

Spanish Fiesta Party

Host a Spanish Fiesta for your invited mehas and mehos. With colourful decorations, Mexican food and festive music, you'll feel like you're in South America, just in time to celebrate Carnival!

Invitations

- Write the party details on small Spanish flags made from paper. Place the flags in envelopes and mail to amigos.
- For fun, include Spanish words on the invitations.

Spanish Cake

- Bake a rectangular cake; cool.
- Decorate the cake with red, white, and green icing to replicate the Mexican flag.
- Add colourful sugar or lolly flowers to the cake.
- Decorate with small Spanish toys that the kids can take home.

Prizes and Party Bags

- Send your amigos home with sombreros, panchos or some castanets.

- Let the kids take home the large paper flowers you used for decoration.

- Give the kids Spanish picture books or cassette tapes of Spanish children's songs.

- Let the kids take home the piñatas they made.

Helful Hints

- Have an interpreter come to the party to translate everything from English to Spanish as the party unfolds.

- If any of your guests have relatives who are Spanish, Mexican or South American, ask them for tips and suggestions to make the fiesta more authentic.

Costumes

- Ask the kids to come dressed in Mexican, South American or Spanish outfits.

- Provide the kids with sombreros, serapes and sandals to add to their ensembles.

- Dress the kids in red, white and green crepe paper when they arrive, creating individual Spanish fashions for each guest.

Decorations

- Make large, colourful flowers from tissue paper, and set them all around the party room.

- Cover the party table in red, white and green paper tablecloths. Add candles to light up the room.

- Hang a large piñata from the ceiling and purchase or make several small piñatas to use as decorations around the room.
- Set out Mexican blankets, bowls, fans, trinkets and other inexpensive decorations.
- Give the room a festive look by making a canopy of streamers in the colours of the Spanish flag.
- Play Spanish music in the background for added atmosphere.

Games

188 Play a version of the Mexican Hat Dance that's more fun and lively than the old-fashioned game. Blow up red, green and white balloons and attach them to ribbons or strings about a metre long. Gather the guests in the party room and tie a ribbon to each player's non-dominant leg. When you say 'Go' have the players try to stomp and pop each other's balloons. At the same time, they should try to keep anyone from popping their balloon!

189 Play the game again, this time tying the balloons to each player's dominant leg, forcing the players to use their non-dominant leg to pop the other player's balloons.

190 Make your own piñatas. They're easy to make when you follow this simple method. First, have each guest blow up a balloon. Tie off the balloons with string and set them on a table covered with newspaper. Pour liquid starch into individual bowls; prepare one for each guest. Place coloured tissue paper on the table and have the kids tear the paper into large pieces or strips. Have the kids dip a piece of tissue paper into the starch, then paste it onto their balloons. Repeat until the balloons are completely covered with several layers of tissue paper. Allow the balloons to dry in the sun. When dry, decorate them with funny or monster faces using permanent felt-tip pens.

191 Make Baker's Clay jewellery. To make Baker's Clay, mix four cups of flour, one cup of salt, and 1½ cups of water, to make a dough. (Add more flour or water as needed, for a smooth, non-sticky consistency.) Let the kids shape the dough into beads, pendants or charms. Use a skewer to make holes for string. Bake at 180°C for an hour, remove from heat, and set aside to cool. When cool, let the kids paint their creations with poster paint or acrylic paint. String with thick embroidery cotton to make necklaces and bracelets.

192 Offer a make-it-yourself taco bar. Include such items as cooked ground beef, varieties of shredded cheese, chopped tomato, shredded lettuce, diced mild green chillies, chopped olives, sour cream and salsa. Give the guests large heated taco shells and let them fill up!

Ages 6–10

Wild West Party

Make the Wild West your theme, and host a rodeo party for the young cowpokes. You can play lots of outdoor games to simulate the Old West and to bring back the fun of the new frontier. So saddle up, young'un, it's time to ride into the sunset.

Invitations

- Send the cowboy and cowgirl guests official 'sheriff' badges. You can buy them at party stores or make them from cardboard cut into stars and covered with foil.

- Write the party details on a 'Wanted' poster, using your special guest of honour as the 'villain'. Attach the sheriff's badge to the poster. Mail in large envelopes.

Sheriff's Star Cake

- Bake two square cakes; cool.
- Cut one cake into five triangles.
- Place the triangles on the sides of the whole cake.
- Cover the cake with icing, and decorate it with the names of heroes from the Old West.

Prizes and Party Bags

- Send the rustlers home with plastic cowboys.
- Give the kids bandanas and belt buckles to wear home.
- Give the kids water-guns to cool off.

Costumes

- Ask the kids to come dressed as cowboys, horseback riders, sheriffs, dance-hall gals or anything related to the Wild West.
- Add bandanas, badges and belt buckles as accessories.

Decorations

- Decorate your backyard to look like a rodeo or ranch.
- Put up 'Wanted' outlaw posters on the fence.
- Hang up lassos and cowboy hats around the party room.
- Create store signs for typical Old West merchants stores, such as blacksmith, livery and dry goods.
- Rope off a 'corral' for the games.
- Set up a stagecoach made from a large cardboard box and an old sheet.

Games

193 Have a lasso contest to see what the kids can round up. Tie a rope into a large circle and have the kids take turns trying to toss it around an inanimate object.

194 Play a one-legged game of tag. Have everyone hop to safety to the other side of the 'corral'.

195 Play a game of horseshoes. Set up a stake in the ground. The players throw horseshoes at the stake. Award one point if the horseshoe lands touching the stake and three points if the horseshoe lands circling the stake. The player with the most points wins. You can make each round harder by moving the players further back each time they have to throw. This game can be played using a horseshoe or quoits set, or kids can make their own horseshoes or quoits out of material such as icy-pole sticks or ice cream container lids.

Ages 6–10

Down on the Farm Party

Say goodbye to city life and gather the young farmers for a day in the barnyard. There's plenty to do down on the farm. So rise and shine, it's farming time!

Invitations

- Cut out pictures of farms from farming magazines and mount them on paper. Write party details around the pictures and mail to guests.
- Fill small boxes with tiny plastic farm animals, write party details on packets of vegetable seeds and mail to guests.
- Send the kids bandanas with the party details written in felt-tip pen around the outside edge.
- Write the party details on gourds and send them in boxes to the kids.

Farm Cake

- Bake a cake, preferably a carrot cake.
- Decorate with chocolate icing.
- Tint shredded coconut green with food colouring and sprinkle over the cake.

163

- Set toy farm animals on one part of the cake and a small farmhouse on another. Create a tiny vegetable garden using small lollies.

Prizes and Party Bags

- Send the farmers home with small farm animals.
- Let the kids keep the accessories—the bandanas, the hats and so on.
- Give each kid a book about farms.
- Make a basket of fruit and give one to each guest.

Variations
- Take a tour of a local farm for an up close and personal look at farming life.
- Visit a petting zoo and let the kids enjoy the animals.

Helpful Hint
- Make sure none of the guests are allergic to animals if you plan to have animals visit the party.

Costumes

- Ask the guests to come dressed as farmers in overalls or jeans and shirts. Provide the accessories when they arrive—neckerchiefs and straw hats.
- Suggest they come dressed as a favourite farm animal for some silly fun.
- Have them wear country dance costumes to the party.

Decorations

- Buy or make your own farm animal posters and hang them on the fence.
- Pile up straw to make a haystack. Use bales of hay for seating around a picnic table.
- Hang a cowbell to call the farmers in when it's meal-time.
- Play square dance music in the background.

Games

196 Animal Antics: For the first round of Animal Antics, sit the kids in a circle. Have each kid draw a card that has the name or picture of an animal on it. The kids take turns making the sound of the animal while the other players try to guess what it is. For the second round, reshuffle the cards and have the kids draw a new animal. Each kid then walks or moves like the animal while everyone guesses what it is.

197 Egg and Spoon Race: Divide the players into two teams and line them up. Give all the players a spoon. Place an egg on the spoons of the first player for each team. Have the kids race back and forth across the yard, holding the egg in the spoon. When they return to their team's line, they must transfer the egg to the next player's spoon—without touching the egg with their hands—so the next player can continue the race. The first team to finish without breaking an egg wins.

198 Taste Test: Seat the players around the picnic table. Place a variety of cut-up fruits and vegetables on the table, covered in foil so they aren't visible. Have the kids close their eyes, then pass around the cut-up foods and let them guess what they are tasting.

Ages 6–10

Hay Ride Party

Hey! Who wants to go to a Hay Ride Party? There's nothing like a hay ride to provide an afternoon or evening of fun, songs and games. So hitch up the wagon—it's time for some horsing around!

Invitations

- Draw hay wagons on the lower halves of sheets of paper. Fold the top halves of the paper over to make covered wagons, glue in some hay and write the party details inside. Mail to guests.
- Tie up small bundles of hay and stick them inside envelopes. Attach party details and mail to guests.
- Cut out pictures of horses and glue them onto paper. Write party details on the back and mail to the guests.
- Write party details on inexpensive bandanas and mail to the guests.

Hay Ride Cake

- Bake a cake and cover with chocolate icing.
- Tint coconut yellow with food colouring and sprinkle over the top of cake to make hay.

- Set a small covered wagon and a couple of plastic horses on top to make a hay ride wagon.

Prizes and Party Bags

- Send the kids home with plastic farm animals or small plastic horses.

- Give the guests bandanas to wear home.

- Let the kids keep their harmonicas.

- Give the kids farmer hats to wear home.

- Buy inexpensive books about horses and pass them out to the kids.

Variation
- Instead of a hay ride, find a local stable and let the kids go horseback riding.

Helpful Hint
- Be sure none of the kids are allergic to hay or animals before they go on the ride.

Costumes

- Ask the guests to wear overalls, jeans or square dance skirts; flannel or plaid shirts; and bandanas as accessories.
- Suggest the kids wear their hair in pigtails or sticking out like Tom Sawyer. Offer to pencil in freckles with a lip liner or makeup pencil when the kids arrive.
- Give the kids farmer hats when they arrive.

Decorations

- Enhance the starting point of your party with bales of hay or a haystack.
- Make a scarecrow to greet the guests by stuffing old clothes with hay. An easy way to prop up the scarecrow is to sit it in a chair.

Games

199 Hay! Watch Out! While you're waiting for the hay ride to start, play this game of skill and balance. Set up some hay bales a couple of feet apart and have the kids try to step from one bundle to the next without falling off. Make it easy to begin with and harder near the end by moving the bundles farther and farther apart.

200 Who's Missing? Have the kids close their eyes. Tap one person to be It and cover him or her in a pile of hay. Tell the rest of the guests to open their eyes and guess who's missing. The first one to yell out the missing player's name gets a point. Repeat with other kids.

201 Harmonica Hayfest: Provide harmonicas to all the guests so they can play some tunes on the hayride. Teach the kids how to play a few simple tunes, such as 'She'll be Coming 'Round the Mountain', 'On Top of Old Smokey (or Spaghetti)', or 'Over the River and Through the Woods'.

202 Hay Painting: Cover the picnic table with newspapers. Give each guest several sheets of white paper. Set out poster paints and sprinkle the table with hay. Have the kids paint their pictures on the paper using the hay as brushes.

203 Scarecrow: Gather some old clothes, accessories, such as eyeglasses, hats, gloves, scarves and jewellery, and lots of hay. Divide the group into teams and have each team create their own scarecrow.

Ages 8–12

Around the World Party

The kids can go around the world without even leaving home when you gather them for a globe-trotting get-together. Fasten your seat belts!

Invitations

- Write the party information on picturesque postcards of other countries. Or make your own postcards by gluing pictures of favourite vacation spots onto stiff cardboard.

- Create paper planes by folding white paper. Unfold the paper and write the party details inside the fold, using such terms as 'arrival and departure times' and 'destination'. Refold, slip each plane into a large envelope and mail.

- Write the party information on the backs of travel posters that depict sites around the world, roll them up and mail in cardboard tubes. (You should be able to find free travel posters at travel agencies.)

Around the World Cake

- Make your favourite cake mix according to packet directions.

- Pour the mixture into a large, well-greased, oven-proof bowl. Bake and cool.

- Carefully loosen the cake from the bowl and place on a cardboard, doily-covered circle.

- Make clouds with white icing, ocean with blue-tinted icing, and earth with chocolate icing—to resemble the Earth from a distance.

- Give the kids poppers filled with little toys from other countries. Fill cardboard tubes with toys, wrap the tubes with crepe paper and tie both ends with ribbon. (Make a bow only, so it can be easily untied.) Fringe the ends of crepe paper with scissors. Let the kids open the poppers to find the surprises inside.

Costumes

- Have the kids dress to represent a particular destination. For example: a snowsuit for Alaska, a Hawaiian shirt for a tropical island, a poncho for Mexico or South America, clogs and braces for the Netherlands or a sari for India. Assign a place or let them pick one themselves.

Decorations

- Transform your home into a setting for your world tour with posters of favourite locations (available at travel agencies).

- Decorate the walls with maps. Use one large map as a tablecloth.
- If you have any items from your world travels, set them around the room, or use them to create a table centrepiece.
- Buy foreign books, magazines and comic books and place them on the tables for guests to enjoy.
- Play world music.

Games

204 Play Pack Your Bags. Fill a suitcase with items from different countries, enough for all guests. Divide the kids into two teams, and have them sit in two lines. Open your suitcase and tell the players you have just returned from a long trip around the world. Give each player an item. To begin the game, the last person in line says the name and the country of origin of his or her item and then passes the item to the next person in line. That person must then repeat the first item and country, then add his or her own and pass both to the next person. The team that finishes first wins the game.

205 Try the Foreign Language game. Find a foreign traveller dictionary with easy-to-say phrases. Choose a simple phrase, such as 'Où est le Louvre?'. Have the kids take turns reading the phrases—and acting them out if they need to—while the rest of the guests try to guess the meaning.

206 Play Travel Puzzle. Glue two travel posters onto two pieces of stiff board. Cut both posters into large puzzle pieces. Divide the players into teams, and have them race to assemble the puzzles—then name the location.

207 Have the kids write to pen pals from other countries. Buy a kids' magazine that lists pen pals. Give each guest stationery and a fancy pen, and have them write to their new foreign friend. Provide comic books and small presents the kids can include with the letters. Drop the letters into the local mailbox.

Science and Nature Parties

Curious kids can explore, discover and delight in these exciting games.

Ages 2–8

Prehistoric Party

A Prehistoric Party comes together faster than you can say Tyrannosaurus Rex! Step into the past, where dinosaurs roamed the party room, and watch the mega-monsters come to life!

Invitations

- Buy large plastic eggs from a hobby or toy store. Cut out pictures of dinosaurs from children's colouring books and write the party details on the backs. Enclose the pictures inside the plastic eggs along with small egg lollies. Decorate the eggs with permanent felt-tip pens or puff paints. Hand deliver or mail the invitations in small, padded boxes.

- Make pop-up invitations that look like eggs with surprise baby dinosaurs inside. Fold a white sheet of paper in half and cut out an egg shape leaving one end of the egg connected. Cut out a small dinosaur picture to fit inside the egg. Fold the dinosaur in half, glue the bottom of the dinosaur to the inside bottom of the egg and the top of the dinosaur to the inside top of the egg. When you open the egg the dinosaur will unfold. Write the party details around the dinosaur. Mail.

Dinosaur Cake

- Bake a rectangular cake; cool.
- Cut the cake in half lengthwise, and lay one half onto a serving plate.
- Using a zigzag cut, slice the remaining half into two large triangles and a number of small triangles to form a dinosaur head, tail and spikes.
- Place the spikes on top of whole half and place large triangles at the head and tail.
- Decorate the cake with green or chocolate icing. Use sprinkles and lollies to create details for face, feet and tail. Serve to carnivores.

Variation
- Take the kids to a museum that features dinosaur exhibits.

Helpful Hint
- Handle the jelly dinosaur eggs carefully so they don't break before the jelly sets!

Prizes and Party Bags

- Create archaeology kits by filling small boxes with compasses, paint brushes, freeze-dried food, rulers and other scientific items so the kids can make discoveries at home.
- Give the kids plastic dinosaurs or books about dinosaurs.

Costumes

- Have the kids come dressed as prehistoric people, cave dwellers, archaeologists or dinosaurs.

- Give the kids sheets of coloured crepe paper, and let them design their own dinosaur costumes at the party.
- Offer the kids props to go with their costumes, such as scientific tools for the archaeologists and bones for the cave people.

Decorations

- Hang up large pictures or posters of dinosaurs.
- Make a volcano from large sheets of paper. Hang it on the wall.
- Set out dry ice to give the room a prehistoric feeling.
- Arrange the furniture in a circle. Drape old sheets and blankets over the furniture to create a cave. Let the kids eat and play games inside the megacave.

Games

208 Play Archaeologist. First, mix two cups of sand, one cup of cornflour and $1^1/_2$ cups of water in a large pan on the stove. Heat the mixture until warm, then shape a handful of the mixture into an egg around a small plastic dinosaur. Allow the egg to dry until firm. Make one egg for each guest and hide the eggs in the yard or party room. Let the explorers hunt for the eggs and break open their discoveries when they find them!

209 Have an archaeological dig. Buy a plastic skeleton, available at science and toy stores, lay the skeleton out on the patio or other surface and cover with dirt or sand. Provide the kids with brushes, and let them gently brush away the dirt or sand to discover the 'fossil'. Have them determine what it is.

210 Play Bone Hunt. Distribute plastic skeleton bones throughout the party room, and let the kids hunt for them. When they find all the pieces, have them work as a team to put the skeleton back together!

211 Make a giant dinosaur in the back yard. Have the kids shape a dinosaur using chicken wire. If throwing this party for younger children, create the dinosaur yourself before the kids arrive. Then let the kids cover the chicken wire with crepe paper to form a dinosaur's body.

212 Cut out large dinosaur shapes from a cardboard box, one for each guest. Let the kids paint their shapes using poster paint. Have a dinosaur parade.

213 Make Dinosaur Jelly Eggs. Cut off the top of an egg, pour it out, and rinse the shell. Make enough for all the guests. Insert a small edible dinosaur or other critter into each shell. Mix jelly according to package directions, and pour into the egg shells. Cool the filled eggs in the refrigerator. After the jelly sets, have the kids crack the eggs open and eat the surprise inside. (Warn the kids to eat carefully, because the jelly contains a surprise.)

214 Make Deep Sea Jelly. Mix blue-coloured jelly, pour it into an aquarium bowl or a large clear bowl and add lolly fish. Allow to set, then serve.

Ages 4–8

Dinosaur Park

Go back to the land before time with a
Dinosaur Park party. During your
expedition, you'll search for fossils, meet
some prehistoric creatures and have a few
exciting adventures along the way!

Invitations

- Buy large plastic eggs at the hobby or toy store.
  Write the party details on small pieces of paper,
  wrinkle the paper, dip in tea, then allow to dry. This
  will give the paper an 'antique' look. Place the paper
  and a small plastic dinosaur inside the eggs and mail
  to the guests in small boxes or padded envelopes.

- Send the kids a dinosaur colouring book. Write the
  party details on each of the pages so they have to
  keep turning pages to read the entire invitation.

Volcano Cake

- Bake cake in a well-greased ovenproof bowl.
  Bake the cake a little longer than called for in the
  directions until it is done in the middle.

- Remove cake from bowl and turn over onto a large
  round plate.

- Decorate the cake with chocolate icing, leaving the top bare.
- Cover the top with red icing, using tubes of icing.
- Stick thin red licorice whips into the top of the cake, shooting out like hot erupting lava.
- Tint shredded coconut green with food colouring and sprinkle around plate. Add plastic toy dinosaurs.

Prizes and Party Bags

- Send the kids home with toy dinosaurs, dinosaur picture or colouring books and dinosaur T-shirts.
- Give the kids a build-it-yourself dinosaur skeleton kit.
- Look around the toy store for anything related to dinosaurs—you're bound to find plenty of fun things to give the kids.

Costumes

- Ask the explorers to come dressed for the expedition as adventurers (like Indiana Jones), scientists in white lab coats (one of the parent's old white shirts) or cave men and women.

Decorations

- Hang up posters of dinosaurs around the yard.

- Set dinosaur toys and stuffed animals on the party table and around the area.

- Cut out jungle trees, giant rocks and a volcano from large sheets of paper and place them on the fence and walls.

- Set up a small scale Dinosaur Park scene using sand, small rocks, toy trees and toy dinosaurs. Use as a centrepiece for the party table.

Games

215 Don't Wake the Dino: Choose one player to be the Dinosaur and have him or her lie down on a towel on the ground. Set plastic eggs with a prize inside all around the Dinosaur. Have the Dinosaur close his or her eyes and pretend to be asleep. One at a time, the players must approach the sleeping Dinosaur and try to steal one of the prize eggs. If the Dinosaur opens his or her eyes and grabs the player, the player becomes the next sleeping Dinosaur and the Dinosaur gets the player's prize.

216 Hot Lava: Create an obstacle path around the yard, using items the kids can step on or climb on, such as a large rock, a small chair, a large shoe, a piece of paper, a short ladder and so on. Set the items close to each other but still challenging to reach. Have the kids cross the yard by stepping only on the items. Anyone who touches the 'hot lava'—or ground—is out.

217 Lost in the Jungle: Blindfold one player and walk him or her to a distant part of the yard. Spin the player around and tell the player to find his or her way back to the rest of the kids. Repeat with all the players, starting them from different parts of the yard. Award prizes to the kids who return to 'civilisation' the fastest.

218 Grow-A-Saurus: Show the kids how to grow their own Dinosaur Plant! Give each guest a knee-high nylon stocking. At the bottom of the stocking, have them pour in a scoopful of lawn seeds. Then fill the stocking with potting soil until the nylon is nearly full, leaving room to tie off the top in a knot. Set the Dino, knot-side-down, into a small plastic bowl. Let the kids glue on wiggly eyes and add a felt cut-out mouth, ears and tail. Gently water the top of the Dino. Tell the kids to take home their Grow-A-Saruses and in a few days their Dinosaur Plants will grow spikes!

219 Let the kids make their own dinosaur skeletons using kits from science or toy stores. Another option is to have the kids design their own dinosaur using icy-pole sticks.

Ages 6–10

Archaeology Expedition

Explore all the possibilities of fun and games on your Archaeology Expedition. All you need is a compass to tell you where to go and a party time machine to get you there!

Invitations

- Draw ancient-looking maps to the party site on cream-coloured paper. When finished, wrinkle the paper and burn the edges to make it look old. Then roll the maps up, place in tubes and mail to all the invited archaeologists.

- Write your party invitations in made-up hieroglyphics. Include a decoder inside the envelope so the guests can decipher the message.

- Send the kids a toy compass with the party details attached.

Pyramid Cake

- Bake a square cake and let cool.
- Cut the cake in half diagonally to form two triangles.

- Ice the tops of both triangles and place them together. Turn the cake on its side to form a pyramid.
- Ice the rest of the cake.
- Using piping bags, add lines around the cake to form ridges.
- Top the cake with a flag, a toy mummy or a candle.

Prizes and Party Bags

- Send the guests home with archaeology tools, compasses and all the goodies they have dug up.
- Give the kids small dinosaur puzzles to put together when they get home.

Costumes

- Ask the guests to come dressed as scientists in white lab coats (large white shirts) or archaeologists in khaki shirts—or provide the shirts to the kids as they arrive.

- Have the guests bring any small tools that might be needed at the dig, such as plastic shovels, magnifying glasses, paintbrushes and so on.

Decorations

- Hang travel posters of the pyramids or other archaeological sites on the fence around the party area.

- Build a small pyramid in the backyard, using cardboard if you want it to be kid-sized or icy-pole sticks if you want it to be a centrepiece.

- Provide a supply of archaeology tools for the guests to use, such as plastic shovels, compasses, maps, paintbrushes, glue and so on. Set the tools on the party table as a centrepiece until it's time to use them.

Variations
- Take the kids to the park so they have a larger area to explore.
- Make a trip to a local museum that houses mummies and other archaeological finds.

Helpful Hints
- Be sure to hide lots of little toys so that everyone finds something while on the expedition.

Games

220 Falling Pyramid: Divide the group into teams. Give each team either a deck of cards, different-sized pieces of cardboard or icy-pole sticks. The teams then have five to ten minutes to build a pyramid that doesn't fall over. The team with the tallest pyramid wins.

221 Fossil Hunt: Buy a bunch of inexpensive plastic insects or dinosaurs. Hide or bury the small toys in the back yard or sandbox. Let the guests collect as many as they can. Let the guests keep what they discover.

222 Mystery Maps: Divide the kids into teams and give each team a map that leads to a buried artifact or hidden treasure. Make each map different, with cryptic clues or picture-graphs, and hide the artifacts in different places, so that each team gets to find a treasure. The first team to find their treasure wins.

223 Ancient Petroglyphs: At the newsagency, buy some antique-looking paper. Pick up a book from the library on petroglyphs and hieroglyphs and photocopy the illustrations so the kids can see them easily. Then provide the kids with felt-tip pens— or paint and brushes—and have them make up their own ancient petroglyphs.

224 King Tut-Tut: Have the kids create their own mummies using toilet paper, crepe paper or torn strips of fabric. Divide the guests into groups and select one kid from each team to be the 'mummy'. Have the teams wrap their mummies in creative ways, then decorate the mummies using felt-tip pens. Award a prize for the Most Creative, the Ugliest, the Scariest, the Cutest and so on.

Ages 6–12

Super Space Party

Take a trip to outer space while the fares
are still cheap! Venture to the Black Hole,
the Milky Way, the planet Mars, and maybe
take a ride on the Starship Enterprise, as
you make your way through the stratosphere.
Fasten your seat belts, it's going to be a
bumpy ride!

Invitations

- Design the invitations to look and read like tickets
  for a Space Shuttle ride from the NASA launch site,
  which just happens to be your house. Mail tickets to
  passengers, along with boarding passes, baggage
  claims and homemade brochures of the destination.

- Send the guests star charts to guide them to your
  home planet—the Party Planet!

- Enclose a package of glow-in-the-dark stars or make
  your own with glow-in-the-dark paint and cardboard
  cut-outs.

Moon Cake

- Bake or buy an angel food cake.
- Cover the cake with fluffy white icing or whipped cream.

- Top the icing with chunks of honeycomb to look like volcanic moon rocks.
- Place a small flag in the centre of the cake to claim the territory.

Prizes and Party Bags

- Give the space explorers books about space.
- Offer freeze-dried food to take home.
- Give the kids glow-in-the-dark stars to put on their bedroom ceilings.

Costumes

- Ask your guests to dress appropriately for the space ride—astronaut costumes or space monsters styles.
- Give the kids headbands or homemade masks of favourite space characters.

Decorations

- Create your own universe in the party room by cutting out cardboard stars and painting them with glow-in-the-dark paint. Hang the stars from the ceiling with ribbon or string. Buy nine different-sized balls, paint them with iridescent paint and hang them from the ceiling to recreate the planets.

- Use Christmas lights with white globes to illuminate the party area.

- Hang posters of the planets and other space charts on the walls.

Games

225 Play Space Exploration. Divide your guests into two teams and give each team a ball of yarn. Send the teams to different parts of the house or yard and have them wind the yarn around various pieces of furniture or plants to create a maze. Have one group try to follow the yarn path through space. If anyone lets go, they will be lost in space forever. When one team finishes, have the other team follow their yarn path.

226 Have a Moon Rock hunt on your new planet. Paint rocks with glow-in-the-dark paint, and hide them around the room. Turn out the lights, then race to see who can collect the most moon rocks for a prize.

227 Make your own Stargazers. Have the kids bring cereal boxes. Paint the containers black, then poke holes in the bottoms in constellation shapes. Give each guest a torch, turn off the lights and have the kids shine the torch into the containers. Aim the bottoms of the containers toward the ceiling. The room should light up with stars!

228 Make Moon Walkers for a challenging trip over the new terrain. Have the kids bring two coffee cans to the party. Paint the cans black, then poke holes near the bottom on either side. String ropes through the holes, leaving one-metre lengths on each side of the cans for the kids to hold. Turn the cans bottom up on the ground. Have the kids step up on the cans and hold onto the ropes. Then have them try to 'walk' on the bumpy terrain using the Moon Walkers.

Ages 7–10

Park Ranger

Let the Park Ranger be your guide to outdoor fun and games. Set up a tent at your favourite local, state or national park then watch out for wildlife as the kids blaze the trails!

Invitations

- Cut out teddy bears from colouring books or draw them on paper. Write the party details on the backs and mail to the guests.
- Get postcards from the park and write the party details on the back.
- Make park ranger badges by covering cardboard stars with foil. Write the guests' names and the party details on the badges using a permanent felt-tip pen.

Teddy Bear Cake

- Bake two round chocolate cakes and eight chocolate cupcakes.
- Lay the two round cakes on the table, one beside the other, to form the bear's head and body.

- Set two cupcakes on either side of the head to form ears, two on either side of the upper body to form arms, two on either side of the lower body to form legs, and one in the centre of the head for the nose.

Variations
- Camp out all night at the park.

Helpful Hints
- Watch out for snakes, spiders, poisonous plants, and other hazards. Pair the kids using the buddy system so they don't get lost.

- Use piping bags of icing and lollies to make eyes, nostrils, mouth, and paws.

Prizes and Party Bags

- Give the kids compasses, small telescopes and maps to take home.
- Buy inexpensive nature books about insects, plants, animals or birds to give to the departing rangers.

Costumes

- Ask the kids to dress as park rangers in khaki shorts or long pants and white or khaki shirts. Give everyone ranger badges when they arrive.
- Encourage the guests to wear hiking boots and backpacks for the trail walks.

Decorations

- Spread checked tablecloths on the picnic tables. Set the table with tin plates and cups.

- Hang park posters around the picnic area.
- Cut out animals from brown cardboard and set them up near the picnic tables.

Games

229 Put one of the adults in a rented animal costume somewhere on the trail. Tell the rangers they have to make it from the start of the trail to the end, without being caught and tagged by the animal, which is hiding along the way! Another option is to simply have an adult act like an animal, such as a kangaroo, without the costume.

230 Lost! Blindfold one of the players and turn him or her around in a circle. The player must find his or her way back to camp area from a short distance away, while the others make distracting animal noises. Once the player reaches the camp area, or gets hopelessly lost, blindfold a different player. The player who reaches camp in the shortest amount of time wins.

231 Park Bingo: Make bingo cards and write down park items in each of the squares, such as a gum nut, a yellow leaf, a dead bug, a smooth stone, a pine needle, a bird feather, a wildflower and so on. Mix up the order of the items and use some different items on each of the cards. Give a card to each ranger and have the kids search the area for the items on their cards. The first one to collect five items in a row wins the game.

232 Camp Collage: Have the kids collect nature items on a trail walk. Bring the items to the picnic table and spread them out. Distribute large sheets of paper to each ranger to create a collage using the items on the table and some glue.

Nature Lovers Party

Mother Nature provides the perfect backdrop for this outdoor party. All you need is green grass to run on and sunshine to play in, then let the kids go wild in the great outdoors!

Invitations

- Collect large leaves and press between two pieces of clear contact paper. Write the party details on top in felt-tip pen and mail to guests.

- Do a leaf rubbing by placing a sheet of paper over a leaf, pressing down on the paper and leaf to keep them in place and gently rubbing a crayon lengthwise over the paper. Write the party details on the back of the paper and mail.

- Cut out a variety of coloured leaves from paper. Write a few of the party details on each leaf then place all the leaves in an envelope and mail. The guests must figure out the correct order of the details before they can read about the party.

Critter Cake

- Bake a cake and cover it with chocolate icing.
- Tint shredded coconut green with food colouring and sprinkle on the cake.
- Make colourful flowers and leaves using piping bags.

Variation
- Take the kids to an arboretum or a botanical garden.

Helpful Hint
- Make sure none of the kids is allergic to things in nature and beware of insects, poisonous plants and other hazards.

- Set lolly bugs, worms and spiders on top.

Prizes and Party Bags

- Send the nature lovers home with plastic bugs and rubber snakes.
- Give the kids magnifying glasses so they can study nature at home.

- Let the guests keep their bug catchers.
- Hand out books on such nature topics as insects, flowers, animals and so on.

Costumes

- Ask the kids to come dressed as park rangers, guides or scouts.
- Send the guests some plastic leaves and ask them to use them in a creative way as part of their costumes.
- Ask the kids to use their imaginations and dress like something in nature, such as a bug, an animal, a plant or a tree.

Decorations

- Mother Nature provides the best decorations, but you can add extra touches by sprinkling plastic bugs, spiders and ants on the picnic table and around the yard.
- Cut out giant coloured leaves and hang them on the fence. Use smaller ones for place mats.
- Hang pictures of wildlife on the fence and walls.

Games

233 Feel the Flora and Fauna: Collect a number of items found in nature, such as a leaf, a bug, a flower, a twig, a rock, some moss, some gum leaves and gumnuts, and a bird feather. Place them in individual paper bags. Gather into a circle and pass around one bag at a time. Have the kids feel inside and try to guess what they are touching. When everyone has guessed, reveal the contents.

234 The 'I Spy' Nature Walk: Make up a list of items found in nature, such as a flower, a leaf, a stone and so on. Pass out the list and have the kids look around the party area or a local park for the items. Whoever finds the most items wins.

235 Plant Parts: Collect parts from various plants—such as the stem of a daisy, an oak leaf and the petal of a rose—and tape them onto a large sheet of paper. Have the kids check the chart, then try to find the matching plant in the yard. Whoever makes the most matches wins.

236 Signs of Nature: Take a nature walk and have the kids pick up any items along the path that do not normally belong in nature, such as old cans, plastic bottles, paper and so on. Give each kid a small paper bag before the walk starts. Whoever picks up the most trash wins.

237 Bug House: Give each child a litre milk carton with the top cut off. Place a number of small, relatively flat nature items on the table, such as flowers, leaves, stems and so on. Cut out pieces of clear contact paper that will fit around each container. Place the contact paper face up in front of each child and let him or her place nature items on top. Leave enough clear space so the contact paper will stick to the container. When the paper is decorated, have the kids wrap it around their containers to make nature-themed boxes. Then cut out circles of netting—each larger than the opening at the top of the containers—and place the netting over the top of the cartons. Secure netting with a rubber band.

Ages 7–12

Garden Party

The backyard garden—whether real or created just for this event—is the foundation for a great outdoor party. There are lots of games and activities to turn all the guests' thumbs green, so dig in!

Invitations

- Buy seed packets from a nursery and write the party details in permanent felt-tip pen on the backs. Enclose in envelopes and mail to the invited gardeners.
- Mail an apple to each guest in a small box. Write the party details on a card and tie it to the stem. Include a recipe for baked apples.
- Buy some artificial flowers and mail them to guests in decorative bunches. Attach a card with the party details.

Flower Cake

- Bake a cake according to packet directions.
- Decorate with white icing.

- Tint shredded coconut green with food colouring and sprinkle all over cake.
- Top with edible flowers or lolly flowers.

Prizes and Party Bags

- Give the kids seed packets to take home.
- Offer the guests a gardening kit consisting of garden gloves, a mist sprayer, seeds and so on.
- Give the guests books on gardening for kids so they can grow things at home.

Costumes

- Ask the kids to come dressed as gardeners or tell them to decorate their clothes with artificial or real leaves and flowers.

Decorations

- Tie paper flowers around the yard.
- Hang large posters of vegetables and fruits.
- Set real or plastic fruits and vegetables on the table. Create a funny monster out of fruits and veggies for the centrepiece.

Variation
- Take the kids to a real community garden. Let them plant or pick real fruits and vegetables.

Helpful Hint
- Check to see if the guests are allergic to any of the foods you will be serving or using for games.

Games

238 Funny Foods: Buy unusual looking foods, such as turnips, bok choy, ginger, celery and so on. Display the items one at a time and have the players guess what each one is. If they don't know, have them make up a funny name for the food item. Award food prizes for the most correct answers.

239 Sweet as a Rose: Buy a variety of fragrant flowers at the florist and put them together in a vase. At game time, have the kids close their eyes. Pull out one flower, pass it around to the players in a circle and have them identify the flower based on its smell. Award prizes for correct answers.

240 Taste and Tell: Cut an onion in half and set it on the table. Gather the kids around the table, blindfold one of them, then give him or her a small piece of a vegetable or fruit to taste. Before tasting the item, the kid must take a whiff of the onion to help disguise the taste. Award prizes for correct answers and repeat with all the kids.

241 Garden Glove Puppet: Give a single garden glove to every guest. Provide a variety of items used in creating finger puppets, such as small pompoms, wiggly eyes, tiny hats, felt, puff paints, felt-tip pens and so on, then let the kids make their own Garden Glove Puppets.

242 Name Garden: Give each guest a flat metal tray, such as a small biscuit sheet or tin box. Fill the tray with a layer of potting soil. Have the kids 'write' their names in the soil using grass seeds. Spray the dirt lightly with water and set in indirect sunlight for the rest of the party, then send them home with the gardeners. In a few days their names will begin to grow!

243 Portable Greenhouse: Draw outlines of greenhouses on green paper. Cut out the centre of each greenhouse, leaving a two centimetre edge around the outside, then distribute the outlines with plastic lunch bags to the kids. Have them moisten a paper towel, fold it in half and place it in the bottom of the bag. Rest five beans or seeds on top of the towel. Tape the cutout greenhouse around the bag, as a frame, then tape the house to a window. Have the guests take their framed bag home and place them on their own windows.

244 Veggie Monster: Place a number of small vegetables and fruits on the table. Ask the kids to create a Veggie Monster, using toothpicks to attach the different pieces of fruits and veggies. Award prizes for the Ugliest, the Most Creative, the Prettiest, the Funniest, the Scariest and so on.

245 Make Garden Face Sandwiches. First make peanut butter and jam sandwiches, then decorate the top of each sandwich with fruits and vegetables cut up to resemble funny faces.

Ages 7–12

Space: The Final Frontier

For the ultimate outdoor party, head for the final frontier—outer space. Host your party at night when the stars are bright and take a journey into the unknown. This party's out of this world!

Invitations

- Buy a packet of glow-in-the-dark stars and planets. Write the party details in permanent felt-tip pen on several of the stars and planets and mail to guests.

- Photocopy a current night sky chart. Rename the stars with the guests' names, then give instructions so each guest can reach the party star.

- Send the invitations via homemade spaceships cut from paper or use small plastic spaceships to send your message.

- Write the party details on black paper using a white paint pen. Use glue-on or stick-on stars as added decoration.

Galaxy Cake

- Bake a round cake and ice it with orange-tinted icing to make it look like the sun.

- Poke thin wooden skewers of varying lengths into large and small marshmallows. Insert the other end of sticks into the cake to make planets. Begin with a small marshmallow set close to the sun for Mercury, and assorted large and small marshmallows for the rest of the planets.

- Paint the marshmallows with food colouring to make the planets more colourful.

Prizes and Party Bags

- Give the kids space or star books to take home.
- Give the guests toy binoculars or telescopes to study the sky.

- Buy some inexpensive space-related toys, such as spaceships, stars, alien figures, and so on, and hand them out to the kids.

Helful Hint
- Choose a clear night for your party so the kids can see the stars and enjoy the night air.

Costumes

- Ask the kids to come wearing space suits or alien costumes.
- Send the guests stick-on stars with the invitations. Ask them to stick the stars on their clothes and faces in a creative way before they come to the party.

Decorations

- Cut out stars from glow-in-the-dark paper (or paint the stars with glow-in-the-dark paint) and stick them around the fences, house and trees. Add a few planets and spaceships, too.
- Cover the table with black paper and place white stars on it with glow-in-the-dark paint or stickers. Make paper plate planets and name each one after a guest, such as 'Planet Tiffany' and 'Planet Jason'.
- Play space-movie music in the background.

Games

246 Alien Invaders: When the guests arrive, attach the same amount of star stickers on each kid's clothes. Once everyone has arrived, pass out cards to each player, with half the cards marked 'alien' and half marked 'earthling'. During the party, the aliens must collect specimens—the stuck-on stars—from the earthlings without being caught. If any alien is caught removing a sticker, he or she must give the earthling who caught them a sticker. The player with the most stickers at the end of the party wins.

247 Flying Saucers: Cut out flying saucers— each the size of a large plate—from heavy cardboard. Cut an eight or ten centimetre hole in the middle of the saucer. Have the kids paint the saucers and decorate them with stickers. Then line up the kids and have them toss their saucers like frisbees across the galaxy (the yard). Whoever sends a saucer flying the farthest wins a prize.

248 Planet Earthywood: Seat three players at a table while the rest of the guests sit on the other side to form an audience. Place a bell or a squeaky toy in front of each player. Read prepared questions about earth and space from index cards; any player who knows the answer rings their bell or squeaks their toy. If it's a correct answer, he or she gets a point. If it's a wrong answer, another player gets a chance to answer. After five points are reached, award a prize and exchange the contestants for a new set of players.

249 Space Ship: Create a giant spaceship from a large appliance box. Let the kids paint it to look like one of the US spaceships, then let them climb in and pretend they're blasting off into space.

Ages 8–14

Science Explorers Party

Let the budding scientists enjoy a party that offers a close-up look at the wonders of the world. Science can be magical, tasty, silly and fun when you create a few amazing experiments. Slip on the lab coats—it's time to explore the mysterious realms of weird science!

Invitations

- Make invitations that appear right before your guests' eyes using this scientific experiment. Use paint brushes or toothpicks to write the party details with milk on white paper. Tell your guests to heat the paper over a candle or in the oven, with adult supervision. The heat will reveal the invitation!

- Write the party information with a white crayon, then have the kids colour over the paper with another crayon to reveal the secret message.

Compass Cake

- Bake two round cakes; cool.
- Cover one cake with icing, top with second cake and cover the entire cake with white icing.

- Using a piping bag, draw a compass face onto the cake, marking north, south, east and west.

Prizes and Party Bags

- Send the scientists home with magnets, compasses, bug collectors, magnifying glasses, kaleidoscopes or the ingredients for slime.

Variations

- Instead of having the party at home, take the scientists on a nature walk and discover new life forms.
- Head for the museum and explore the world of dinosaurs, early man or other science-related adventures.
- Instead of a Compass Cake make a Rock Cake. Bake a chocolate cake filled with nuts and marshmallows, cover with chocolate icing and top with 'rock' candy.

Helpful Hint

- Tell the kids that experimenting with science can be dangerous and warn them to use caution and adult supervision when exploring.

- Give the kids small books on famous scientists.
- Offer the kids easy-to-do scientific experiments to take home.

Costumes

- Buy some men's white shirts at a second-hand shop and use them as lab coats for your guests. Write their scientist names on one pocket, such as Dr Frankenstein with a permanent felt-tip pen.
- Offer the kids goofy glasses and wild ties to go with their outfits and tuck some pens into their pocket protectors.

Decorations

- Place jars full of coloured water on the table and run hoses from one jar to another to look like experiments.

- Set dry ice in the centre of the table so the steam creates a weird bubbling experiment.

- Cut out question marks from black paper and tape them to the walls or hang them from the ceiling with string.

- Borrow microscopes, chemistry sets, magnifying glasses, compasses and so on, and place them on the table and all around the party room.

Games

250 Before the party, take close-up pictures of everyday items. Develop the pictures, glue them onto coloured paper and draw a magnifying glass around each picture, so they look as though they are being viewed through a magnifier. Have the kids examine the pictures and try to guess what everyday items are represented. Since the items have been enlarged, identifying them should be a challenge.

251 Cut celery stalks and set them in glasses of water tinted with food colouring. Let the celery stalks soak up the coloured water, remove them from the glasses and serve to the kids with cream cheese or peanut butter.

Ages 8–14

Planet Earth Party

Celebrate the planet with a Planet Earth Party. Combine science, nature, and creativity, and you'll find a world full of curious fun and games!

Invitations

- Send postcards of the planet Earth with the party details as the message.
- Make your own postcards by attaching magazine pictures of the Earth to index cards.
- Attach small plastic globes to the invitations, and mail them in small, recyclable boxes. (Globes are available at toy stores.)
- Write the party details on packets of flower or vegetable seeds using a black, permanent, felt-tip pen; mail to your guests.

Flower Cake

- Bake a cake; cool.
- Decorate the cake with chocolate icing.
- Sprinkle crushed chocolate biscuits on the icing to look like dirt.

216

- Top the cake with real or artificial flowers that appear to 'grow' out of the cake. (If using real flowers, use edible varieties available at many grocery and specialty stores.)
- Add a few lolly worms for even more fun!

Variations

- Take the kids on a nature walk and point out environmental issues, topics, activities and so on.
- Visit a museum and have the tour guide talk about the environment.

Helpful Hint

- Don't turn the party into a work day—keep it fun and interesting, while learning to keep the Earth clean and healthy.

Prizes and Party Bags

- Give the kids packets of flower or vegetable seeds to take home and plant.
- Offer gardening tools wrapped with ribbon.
- Have the kids take home the pressed flowers and flower pots they made.

Costumes

- Ask the kids to come dressed as scientists, explorers or naturalists.
- Provide the kids with camouflage shirts or ties, and men's large, old, white shirts for lab coats.
- Ask the kids to come dressed as something from the earth itself—and leave the costumes to their imaginations!

Decorations

- Decorate the party room with posters of the Earth, the stars, the environment—anything that has to do with the planet.

- Hang stars from the ceiling, cut out trees from paper and tape them to the walls and draw a mural of the horizon.

- Set out globes of the Earth, charts and maps, aerial photographs and other views of our world.

Games

252 Have a Litter Race. Divide the kids into teams and give each team a paper bag. Give the kids a ten minute time limit to collect as much litter in the neighbourhood as they can. When all the kids return, count or weigh the litter and award a prize.

253 Make a Tiny Terrarium. Save large, clear, plastic soft drink bottles—you'll need one for each guest. Cut the tops off the bottles, leaving about 13 centimetres on the bottom. Discard the tops. Give the kids the plastic bottoms and have them fill the bottles with dirt and plant seeds. Or have the kids layer tiny rocks or sand in the bottoms to create earth layers. Provide small plastic figures and tiny artificial plants to create miniature scenes.

254 Create colourful sand designs. Colour the sand by placing sand in bowls and rubbing the sand in each bowl with coloured chalk—each bowl a different colour. The chalk will disintegrate, colouring the sand. Have the kids pour the coloured sand in layers. Finish by decorating the sand with artificial flowers.

255 Make pressed flowers. Give each kid a flower, a thick book and two sheets of wax paper. Have them place one sheet of wax paper into the middle of the open book. Tell them to place the flower on top of the wax paper and to arrange the petals any way they like. Then have them carefully place the second sheet of wax paper over the flower and close the book. Leave the flower in the book for at least 30 minutes before removing it.

256 Create decorative flower pots. Give each guest a plastic pot, fabric scraps, glitter, stickers, ribbons and puffy paints. Let the kids decorate their pots.

Crazy Circus Parties

Get the Big Top ready for some amazing acts that will have the kids in hysterics!

Ages 2–12

Carnival/Circus Party

The circus is coming to town and it's bringing a party with it! Turn your house, yard or garage into a big top celebration, with lots of goodies, games and kooky clowns. It's carnival time for kids of all ages!

Invitations

- Make clown masks using paper, felt-tip pens, sequins and glitter. Use a glue gun or super glue to attach a red rubber ball for a nose, then cut out eye holes. Tie a string to either side of each mask, write the party details on the inside of masks, and mail them in large envelopes.

- Insert invitations into boxes of circus animal biscuits. Place each box of biscuits into another small box to keep the biscuits from being crushed in the mail.

Buried Clown Cake

- Bake a cake; cool.
- Decorate the cake with chocolate icing.

- Make Clown Cones: Scoop round balls of ice cream into sugar cones; turn the cones upside down onto a plate and decorate the ice cream clown faces with piping bags using the cone as the clown's hat. Keep in freezer until cake time.

- When ready to assemble, place Clown Cones on top of the cake, ice cream side down, evenly spaced, one for each guest, so the clowns look as though they are buried beneath the cake and only their heads are sticking up.

Variations

- Go to the circus if it's in town and enjoy a real big top and Ferris wheel. (Be sure to have enough adult supervision.)
- Find out when your local communities are hosting festivals and make one of those events the focus of your party.

Helpful Hints

- Be sure to have lots of prizes on hand for the games—for both winners and losers—so everyone has a good time and feels successful!
- Have the kids win tickets instead of toys at the carnival booths, then have them cash in the tickets for a prize at the end of the party.

Prizes and Party Bags

- Send the kids home with small stuffed animals you'd find at a circus.
- Make popcorn balls and give them to the kids to take home.
- Let the kids keep the small toys they win at the game booths.

Costumes

- Ask your guests to come dressed as clowns! Suggest they dress in colourful, baggy second-hand shop clothes. Decorate their faces with face paint.
- Have the kids dress like circus animals or as one of the side-show characters.
- Award costume prizes for Funniest, Most Creative, Scariest, Saddest and so on.

Decorations

- Make your own big top tents by hanging sheets and blankets or paper streamers from the ceiling.
- Create carnival game booths using large cardboard boxes painted with poster paint.
- Fill the party room with multicoloured balloons for a festive atmosphere.
- Place stuffed animals and clown dolls around the party room for an added attraction.
- Distribute items used in a circus, such as hoops, nets, batons and so on, throughout the party room.

Games

257 Have the party 'animals' do some circus stunts, taking turns being the ringmaster who gives orders. The kids can jump through hoops, leap over ropes, duck under sticks and step through tyres and other obstacles while behaving like animals.

258 Play carnival games using the cardboard-box booths. Include such games as Ring the Soft Drink Bottle with rings cut from cardboard; Gone Fishin' with sticks, string and magnets for fishing poles; Penny Platter with coins tossed on a plate; Catch a Goldfish with real goldfish in a kiddy pool that the kids try to catch with their hands; and Water Gun Shooting Gallery with squirt guns to shoot small plastic bottles off a ledge.

259 Have each kid draw a clown face on a large sheet of paper using felt-tip pens, crayons or paint. See who can come up with the funniest face.

260 If the kids don't come with their faces already painted, have them use face paint to decorate each other's faces to look like clowns.

261 Instead of having the kids wear costumes to the party, provide a variety of funny, old, second-hand shop clothes at the party and have them mix and match to create their own crazy clown look.

262 Make Animalwiches by cutting animal shapes out of bread with cookie cutters. Fill with favourite spreads.

263 Cut out slices of bread, cheese and meat using animal cookie cutters. Place all animal shapes on a platter and let the kids assemble their animal sandwiches as they would a puzzle.

Ages 5–10

Circus Party

Come one, come all, to the greatest show on earth—the Circus Party! There will be lots of big top fun and clowning around. So step right up, one and all. The show is about to begin!

Invitations

- Find a picture of a clown in a colouring book and reproduce it for your guests. Glue spongy clown noses (available at party and costume stores) to the faces. Write party details on the backs of the drawings and mail to the guests.

- Draw a circus poster with the party details in the headlines and in the small print. Add a picture of the guest of honour with a clown nose attached. Mail to the guests.

Variation
- Take the kids to a real circus.

Helpful Hint
- Don't overdo the sugar. Be sure to give the kids a balanced meal before they eat too many of the goodies.

- Buy a packet of tiny plastic circus animals or clowns, attach a note with the party details to each toy and mail in small boxes to the guest.

Clown Face Cake

- Bake a round cake and cover with white icing.
- Decorate top to make a silly clown face, using jellybeans, sprinkles, coloured marshmallows and licorice.
- Let the kids make their own clown face cupcakes by providing a supply of icing, gels, sprinkles and other edible decorations.

Prizes and Party Bags

- Give the guests tiny circus animals to take home for their own circus fun.
- Let the kids have a supply of face paints so they can make their own clown faces.
- Purchase small clown dolls and give one to each guest.

- Send the kids home with a popcorn ball, a bag of peanuts, or a caramel apple.

Costumes

- Ask the kids to come dressed as clowns, circus performers, ringmasters, animals or acrobats.

Decorations

- Stick a pole in the middle of the yard and drape a sheet over the top. Pull the ends out and attach them to trees or fences to make a big top circus tent.

- Instead of using a sheet, create the feeling of a big top with crepe paper streamers by hanging them from the centre of the party area to the outside. Twist the streamers and use different colours for a festive look.

- Get large boxes and paint them to resemble animal cages. Cut out long slits along one side to make bars for the cage. Place large stuffed animals inside.

- Fill the area with balloons or tie the balloons together to make a big top tent.

- Make a three-ring circus by placing lengths of rope in circles on the ground. Make sure the circles are large enough for the kids to perform inside.

Games

264 Lion Taming: Have the players form a circle, facing in toward the middle—they are the lions. Choose one kid to be the ringmaster and have him or her walk around the outside of the lions' circle. The ringmaster must tag a lion, then run around the ring and make it back to where the lion was standing before the lion touches him or her. If the ringmaster makes it back, he or she is a lion. If not, he or she is 'eaten' and is out of the game. Play until only one kid remains.

265 Awesome Acrobats: Borrow some mats from a local gym or make your own from old mattress pads, air mattresses or foam blocks. Let the kids do acrobatic stunts, such as tumbling and cartwheels in a follow-the-leader pattern.

Ages 5–12

Carnival Time

Your own backyard is the perfect place to host a carnival party. Let the whole family help prepare for the guests by making the booths and planning the games. It's Carnival Time!

Invitations

- Cut out giant tickets from paper, using real tickets as models. Write the party details on the tickets, stuff into large envelopes and mail to guests.

- Buy a roll of tickets from a party store, rip off a half dozen or so for each guest, then write the party details on the tickets. Tear the strips into individual tickets, mix them up, place in envelopes and mail.

- Insert a small carnival toy—such as a plastic whistle, a finger-trap or a tiny puzzle—inside the envelopes.

Carousel Cake

- Bake two round layer cakes. Stack them on top of each other. Decorate with white icing.

- Stick peppermint sticks in a circle on the cake to form a carousel.

- Set tiny toy animals next to the peppermint sticks.

Prizes and Party Bags

- The kids should have lots of small prizes to take home.

- Give the kids a goody bag filled with surprises that they can't open until they get home.

Variation

- Invite the kids to help set up the carnival one day then enjoy it the next day.

Helpful Hint

- Make sure there are lots of prizes for both winners and losers.

Costumes

- Ask the kids to dress like carnival workers.

- Make special carnival shirts using inexpensive T-shirts and puff paints. Write the guests' names on the backs.

Decorations

- Collect large boxes to use as carnival booths, then paint the boxes with poster paint. Add flowers, stars and other designs for detail. Set the booths in a semicircle in the yard.

- Decorate the fence, back yard and house with crepe paper streamers to make the area festive. Add balloons to the booths for colour and fun.

- Hang posters with carnival slogans on the fence, such as 'Guess Your Weight', 'Ten Throws for 10 cents', and 'Win a Prize!'.

- Play carnival or marching band music in the background.

Games

266 Balloon Pop: Write the names of different prizes on small pieces of paper and roll them up into little tubes. Blow up enough balloons for all the guests, insert one slip of paper into each balloon, then tie off the balloons. Have the players sit in a circle around the balloons. Blindfold one player and let him or her try to find and pop a balloon by stomping on it. When the balloon pops, remove the blindfold and read the name of the prize. Repeat with all of the kids.

267 Bottle Ring: For this classic carnival game, set up 12 bottles on a platform, four across by three down. Cut out rings from heavy cardboard, making sure the rings are large enough to easily fit around the necks of the bottles. Let the kids try to toss the rings over the bottle necks to win prizes.

268 Guess How Many: Count out a large number of small lollies and place them in a jar. The guest who guesses the actual number of lollies wins the jar and the lollies.

269 Nosy the Clown: Paint one booth to look like a giant clown face. Cut a circle where the nose should be, large enough to toss a beanbag through. Give prizes to the kids who toss the most beanbags through the nose.

270 Penny Toss: Place a number of empty containers of varying sizes—such as a tuna can, a juice can and so on—on a platform. Set the cans up in random order, assigning each one a point value based on difficulty. Give the players ten coins and let the kids try to toss them into the cans. Award different prizes for different point totals.

271 Go Fishing: Line up all the kids at the Fishing Pond Booth. Hand the first fisherman a pole and have him or her throw it into the 'pond' behind the booth. Tie a prize to the end of the line. Pull up the line and let the kid discover the prize!

272 Grab Bag: Paint one of the booths black and call it the Black Hole Booth. Hide wrapped prizes inside the booth. Let the kids reach into the Black Hole one at a time and grab a prize.

Crack-up Comedy

Crack up the crowd with jokes and jests
and crazy antics!

Invitations

- Fold three sheets of paper together.
- Staple them at the fold to make a booklet with
  six leaves (12 pages).
- On the front of the booklet write 'Knock! Knock!'
- On the second leaf write 'Who's there?'
- On the third leaf write 'Boo!'
- On the fourth leaf write 'Boo who?'
- On the fifth leaf write 'Why are you crying when
  you could be laughing at my Crack-Up Comedy
  party?'
- Write the party details on the last leaf, and illustrate
  the invitations with cartoon drawings.

Hamburger Cakes

- Squirt a bit of yellow, red and green icing onto the flat sides of two vanilla wafers to resemble mustard, tomato sauce and lettuce.
- Press a chocolate biscuit between the vanilla wafers to resemble a hamburger between two buns.
- Dot the top of the 'bun' with white icing to make sesame seeds.

Prizes and Party Bags

- Joke books
- Funny glasses, clown feet, giant noses and other gag accessories
- Fake vomit, rubber insects and other gag gifts

Costumes

- Ask the cut-up clowns to bring their favourite jokes. Have them accessorise their clothes with funny items like big hats, Groucho glasses or giant rubber feet.

Decorations

- Make a comedy stage by hanging bed-sheet curtains across a corner of the room.

- Make a sign announcing the comedians appearing at the party and place it near the stage.

- Cut out celebrity smiles from magazines and tape them to the walls.

- Set the table with gag gifts like fake vomit, rubber chickens and whoopee cushions.

- Place a smile cut-out at each place setting.
- Provide funny costume accessories, such as giant underwear, red noses, wild wigs and false teeth.

Games

273 Hats: Collect a variety of hats and place them in a box. Have the players stand in a circle around the hats. The group must think of a theme for the game, such as 'asking someone to dance' or 'applying for a job'. Players close their eyes and each pulls out a hat. Go around the circle and have each player incorporate his or her hat into a theme-related skit. For example, if the theme is 'asking someone to dance' and someone picks a cowboy hat, they might say, 'Howdy, pardner, would you like to do the two-step at the OK Corral'.

274 Rap: On separate slips of paper, write potentially funny situations like 'late for school', 'got mosquito bite', 'lost a jacket', and so on. Give each player a situation and have the players take turns making up raps to their themes. Or let all the kids make up a progressive rap, with each player contributing a line.

275 Let guests take turns telling jokes onstage. Pass around a joke book and have guests take turns reading jokes. Write a bunch of riddles or jokes on small slips of paper and write the punch lines on separate slips. Mix up the slips and have players try to match the jokes with their punch lines.

276 Have one player lie face-up on the floor. A second player also lies face-up, head on the first player's tummy. The next player does the same, until all players are lying down with their heads on other players' tummies. Have the first player say 'Ha!' Have the second player say 'Ha! Ha!' Repeat, with each player adding an extra 'Ha!' each time, until the whole group is laughing uncontrollably!

Ages 10–14

Custom Circus

Host an evening of fun and games under the Big Top!

Invitations

- Find a photo of your child. Have copies made.
- Fold white paper in half.
- Glue the photo onto the right inside page of the card. Write party details around the photo.
- Cut a hole in the front of the card so the photo shows through when the card is closed.
- Tape a small piece of clear cellophane over the cutout on the inside of the card.
- Using permanent markers in a variety of colours, draw clown-face makeup on the front of the cellophane so that when the card is closed, the photo is disguised to look like a clown.
- When the card is opened, your child's face and the party details are revealed.

Popcorn Clown Cakes

- Melt 40 marshmallows with ½ cup of butter in a large pan.
- Pour over seven cups of popped popcorn in a large bowl.
- Divide among the guests and have them shape the popcorn with buttered hands to make flat, round faces.
- Decorate with icing to make clown faces.

Prizes and Party Bags

- Inflated balloons with small toys inside
- Miniature clown dolls
- Face-painting kits
- Books about the circus
- Large containers of popcorn
- Stuffed animals

- Ask each kid to bring a stunt to perform at the party.

Decorations

- Tape many long, colourful crepe paper streamers to the centre of the ceiling. Twist them and tape them to the wall about half a metre below the ceiling, leaving long ends dangling to the floor. Twist the ends and tape them to the edges of the floor. Make sure the entire room is enclosed in crepe paper for a dazzling tent-like effect!

- Inflate balloons with helium and tie a piece of colourful curling ribbon to each. Let the balloons float up to the ceiling with their ribbons hanging down.

- Make a balloon archway at the entrance to the party room.

- If you can get photos of the guests in advance, take them to a copy shop and enlarge them, then colour the faces with markers to make clownish disguises. Tape the photos to the wall.

- Cover the table with a colourful crepe-paper tablecloth. Make a balloon centrepiece and serve food in festive paper tableware.

Games

277 Place a rope on the floor and wind it around the room, making turns and loops. Have guests try to walk the tightrope without stepping off. To make the game more challenging, lay the rope in a straight line and have guests walk the tightrope with their eyes closed!

278 Make a circus ring out of rope. Choose one guest to be the Ring Master, who announces each act. Have the guests take turns performing the stunts they prepared at home. They can juggle balls, spin paper plates on their fingers, 'tame' stuffed tigers and lions and much more.

279 Have guests remove their slippers and place them in a path going from one end of the room to the other, 30 centimetres apart. Guests must then try to walk the path, stepping only on the slippers.

280 Have guests line up on one side of the party room, standing in their sleeping bags. At the word 'Go!' have them race to the other side of the room! Anyone who falls down is out of the game.

281 Have guests make up each other's faces with face paint. Or have guests paint their own faces. Set up a Polaroid snapshot booth and take photos of all the clowns, who then get to keep the photos.

Drama Parties

Kids who like to dress up, act and be stars will love these theatrical parties!

Ages 2–10

Action Heroes Party

Superman or Supergirl, Mega Man or Mighty Morphins—whatever your child's favourite superhero, celebrate the favourite character at an Action Heroes Party! Then let the kids power-up, conquer evil and save the day!

Invitations

- Cut action hero emblems and logos from felt. Cut out the same logos from double-sided iron-on interfacing paper. Iron the two layers together. Mail the logos and the party details to your guests. Tell the guests to ask their parents to iron the logos onto old T-shirts or capes and to wear them to the party.

- Make a copy of a page from an action hero comic book, white out some of the speech bubbles, fill in the party details, make copies and mail to guests.

Action Hero Cake

- Bake a cake; cool.
- Decorate the cake with an emblem from your child's favorite action hero costume, such as Superman, using appropriately coloured icing.

- Set action figures all over the cake. Give these to the kids after the party.

Prizes and Party Bags

- Send the action heroes home with small plastic action figures and comic books.

Variation
- Have an adult friend come to the party in costume for a surprise visit.

Helpful Hint
- Include a list of action heroes on the invitations to stimulate creative choices; some ideas are Wonder Woman, Super Girl, Mighty Mouse, Green Hornet, Spider Man, Flash Gordon, Cat Woman, The Joker, The Riddler and Atom Ant.

- Hand out the Power Portraits and capes the kids made during the party.

Costumes

- Have the kids dress up as action heroes.
- Supply kids with masks, capes, gloves, glasses or other accessories.

Decorations

- Set the super scene by creating or buying giant cut-outs of action heroes and hanging them on the walls.
- Play theme songs from popular action hero shows.
- Make table centrepieces and decorations with small plastic action figures and comic books.

Games

282 Host an Action Hero Olympics. Prepare a series of challenging feats, varying the games so that everyone has a chance to win. Offer some group games so that large numbers of kids will win, too. Include weightlifting, long jumping, fast running, long-distance ball throwing, balance-beam walking, obstacle course challenges and relay races.

283 Play Super Hearing. Have the kids identify mysterious recorded sounds.

284 Play Super Tasting. Blindfold the kids and have them sample and guess foods.

285 Play Super Smelling. Blindfold the kids and have them sniff a variety of aromas and name the sources.

286 Play Super Vision. Have the kids look at enlarged or reduced pictures of everyday items and guess what they are.

287 Make Power Portraits. On paper, trace and cut out two body outlines of each guest. Have the kids decorate the outlines—one as the front and the other as the back—using felt-tip pens, scraps of fabric, puffy paints and glitter. Staple the sheets of paper together, leaving an opening at the top. Stuff the 'bodies' with newspaper, then seal the head and prop up the heroes around the party room or table.

288 Make your own action hero comic books. Have each guest draw and colour a panel featuring his or her favourite action hero character. Assemble the panels to make a funny story.

289 Make fabric capes. Have the kids decorate the capes with glitter and stars.

290 Build a superhero sandwich. Buy two long loaves of bread and cut off one end of each. Fill the loaves with layers of meat, cheese, tomato and lettuce. Place the sliced ends together to create a superlong sandwich!

Ages 8–12

Gladiator Games

Hercules and Xena are here to help you make your Gladiator Games Party a glorious success. Test the strength and endurance of your guests as they play the parts of mighty men and wonder women.

Invitations

- Find postcard-sized pictures of gladiators, photos of Hercules and Xena, superheroes, or pictures of famous wrestling stars. Write your party details on the backs of the pictures and mail to guests.

- Buy high energy bars for the guests, attach a card with the party details, and invite them to the Gladiator Games.

- Prepare fill-in-the-blank scorecards for the games and mail with the party details. Beside each guest's name write 'Winner!'

Gladiator Arena Cake

- Make a cake and decorate with green icing.
- Set tiny figurines on top, such as Hercules and Xena, gladiators, superheroes or wrestlers.

- Give action and stunt poses to the figures on the cake.
- Add gold coins around the outside for a sparkling decoration.

Helpful Hint
- Make sure the losers also receive fun prizes.

Prizes and Party Bags

- Give the kids medallions, ribbons, trophies, medals and other awards based on the number of points they earned playing the games.
- Offer posters of the kids' heroes to take home. Give them the figures from the cake.

Costumes

• Ask the kids to come dressed as their favourite superheroes, gladiators or as Hercules and Xena.

• If you prefer, have the kids dress in sport clothing or tracksuits so they can play the games easily and not worry about their costumes.

Decorations

• Buy posters of the gladiators, Hercules and Xena, and favourite superheroes and post them on the fence and side of the house.

• Set up trophies on the table. Mark each place setting with a red ribbon.

• Write out scorecards on large sheets of cardboard, listing the names of the games and the contestants. Post the cards so everyone can see them.

• Dress up the back yard with colourful streamers and balloons to make a festive arena for play.

Games

291 Blind Walk: Test the kids' bravery with a Blind Walk. Create an obstacle path from one end of the yard to the other. Line up the contestants and let them have a good look at the path. One at a time, blindfold the gladiators and have them walk the path without looking. Note each player's time on the scorecard.

292 Gold Coin Toss: Test the kids' arm strength and depth perception. Buy a bunch of chocolate gold coins. Set a small bucket in the middle of the yard and have the gladiators line up about four metres from it. One at a time, let each player try to toss ten gold coins into the bucket. Award one point for each coin that goes in. Let each player keep the coins that make it into the container.

293 Hacky Sack: Test the kids' flexibility and coordination. Divide the group into pairs; give each pair a hacky sack. On the word 'Go' have the pairs pass the hacky sack back and forth using their feet. Award points to the pair that lasts the longest without letting their hacky sack touch the ground. Repeat several times.

294 Tug of War: Test the group's strength. Divide the players into two teams. Have the teams stand in a line opposite each other, about 1^1/$_2$ metres apart. Place a long rope in the centre, giving the ends to each team. On the word 'Go' have the teams try to pull one another across a middle line. Award points to all the players on the winning team.

295 Rope Walk: Test the kids' balance. Lay a thick rope out on the yard, curving it around in a maze-like fashion. Have the gladiators walk along the rope. Mark points off each time they lose their balance and step off the rope.

296 Gladiator Garb: Make Gladiator accessories for the kids' costumes by having them create their own wrist and ankle bands. Let them cut out strips of coloured felt, wrap the strips around their wrists and ankles and use self-sticking Velcro to secure them. Make sweatbands the same way.

297 Mystery Masks: Cut masks out of stiff cardboard. Let the kids decorate the masks using fabric pieces, sequins and glitter, felt-tip pens, feathers and glue. Have the guests give themselves mysterious names to match their masks.

Ages 8–12

Hollywood Stunts

Spend a day in Hollywood for some
behind-the-scenes action and fun. Show the
kids how those miraculous movie stunts and
tricks happen. Lights, camera, action!

Invitations

- Buy postcards of famous action stars from
  Hollywood, such as Jackie Chan, Xena, Hercules
  and so on, or buy postcards of stunt scenes from
  movies. Write the party details on the backs and
  mail to guests.

- Make your own invitations that will surprise and amaze your guests. Cut rectangles from stiff white paper and fold in half to make

Helpful Hint
- Watch the kids carefully as they perform their stunts so they don't get carried away and do anything dangerous.

cards. On separate sheets of paper, cut out stars that are a little smaller than the size of the folded cards. Write 'Hollywood Stunt Party' in the centre of the stars; write the party details around the inside edges of the folded cards. Colour the stars and add glitter. Cut out small rectangles of paper and fold the two ends in a zigzag. Glue the stars to the tops of the strips, then glue down the ends of the strips to the inside centres of the cards. Fold the cards, carefully pressing down the stars. When the cards are opened the stars will jump out at the readers.

Stunt Cake

- Bake a cake and decorate with a favourite icing.
- Decorate the cake with stars using a piping bag.
- Cut pieces for all the kids and place on plates.
- The kids must eat their cake without using their hands or cutlery.

Prizes and Party Bags

- Send the kids home with stunt books and collecting cards from action movies.

Costumes

- Ask the kids to come dressed in shorts and T-shirts, athletic tracksuits or other flexible clothes.
- Have the kids come dressed as a favourite action movie star.

Decorations

- Decorate the party area with cut-out stars featuring action words such as 'Pow', 'Blam', 'Wham' and so on. Use a few of the stars as personalised place mats by writing the kids' names on them.
- Hang posters of famous movie action scenes.
- Play music from action movies such as 'Indiana Jones' or 'Hercules'.

Games

298 Binocular Walk: Have the kids walk an obstacle course while looking through the wrong end of a pair of binoculars. Award prizes for the kids who complete the course in the best time.

299 Do-It Dice: Make a giant pair of dice by taping together six equal-sized squares of cardboard per die. Write a stunt on each side of the dice, such as 'Hop on one foot', 'Walk backwards' and so on. Have the players take turns rolling the dice and then acting out the required stunts. For example, if one die rolls up 'Hop on one foot' and the other rolls up 'Sing the alphabet backwards', the player must do both stunts at once.

300 Falling Statues: Have two players stand on flat squares of cardboard placed a metre apart. Give each kid opposite ends of a rope and have them try to pull each other off their cardboard squares. Whoever falls off first loses the bout. Repeat with all the kids until one kid is crowned as the grand champion.

301 Hula Hoopers: Give the kids Hula Hoops and have them perform designated tricks, such as 'Hula Hoop in slow motion', 'Hula Hoop super fast', 'Use your neck', 'Try your arms' and so on.

302 Leapin' Limbo: Have the kids jump over a stick as it rises higher and higher, then have them limbo under the stick as it gets lower and lower. Anyone who touches the stick is out.

303 Divide the kids into two teams and let them design a stunt for the other team. Have the first team show how to do the stunt, then have the second team do it—if it can.

Ages 8–14

Creative Careers Party

Take a look into the future to see what the kids will be when they grow up. Give them a chance to come as anyone they want to be— teachers, doctors, astronauts, dog catchers, rock stars, police officers, even leaders! It's time to get a job!

Invitations

- Mail the kids job application forms you've designed yourself, using a real application as a model. Substitute party questions here and there, such as 'Are you available to party from 2 pm to 4 pm on Friday?'

- Send the guests a copy of the classified ads from the newspaper, adding your own 'party ad' in the middle of the listing. Have it read something like this: 'Wanted: party attendee, willing to eat large quantities of cake and ice cream, play silly games, and have tons of fun. Send RSVP, résumé ASAP.'

Briefcase Cake

- Bake a rectangular cake; cool.
- Decorate the cake with chocolate icing.
- Cut fruit roll-ups into a handle shape to create a handle.
- Add the birthday child's initials (or the initials of the guest of honour) in yellow icing as a monogram (and add Happy Birthday for a birthday cake).
- Try other designs, such as a blackboard for a teacher, a space ship for an astronaut, or a star-shaped cake for a rock star.

Variation

- Instead of staying home for the party, take the kids out to explore new career opportunities. Visit the zoo to find out what it's like to be an animal trainer, a factory to see how things are made, or a fire station to see the firefighters on the job.

Helpful Hint

- When you send out invitations, send the kids ideas for career choices to stimulate their creative juices.

Prizes and Party Bags

- Send each guest home with a book about jobs.
- Give each kid a key chain to start a collection of keys.
- Hand out address or appointment books.
- Give each kid one of the hats used for decorations.

Costumes

- Have the kids come dressed in outfits that represent their favourite occupations.
- Tell the kids to come dressed as what they want to be when they grow up.
- Suggest that the kids find items at a second-hand shop to create their costumes.
- Send each kid a hat and have the kid create a costume to go with it.

Decorations

- Decorate the party room with items that represent different careers. Hang a stethoscope from the ceiling to represent a doctor, place a briefcase on the table for a lawyer, stick alphabet posters to the wall for a teacher and put up pictures of rock stars for the future singers.
- Display a collection of hats from various careers. You may have a fire hat, police hat, sailor hat, detective hat, baseball hat, builder's hard-hat and army helmet. You can find hats at second-hand shops, costume shops and party shops.

Games

304 Collect a variety of clothes and accessories that represent a number of occupations and place the items in individual bags or suitcases. Choose some obscure careers as well as some obvious ones to make the game interesting. Have one player choose a bag and try on one article of clothing, then have the other players try to guess what he or she is supposed to be. If the kids can't guess, have the player add another article or accessory until someone finally guesses the correct occupation. Some ideas for career outfits include pizza maker, pool cleaner, dog groomer, fashion model, electrician, window cleaner, dance instructor, grave digger, bank teller and garbage collector.

305 Before the party begins, collect several large boxes. Cut off the tops and bottoms of the boxes, cut along one side, then open the boxes into four panels. Be sure there is one panel for each guest. Draw a basic outline of a person on each panel. Cut out the face area. Have each guest paint a panel, giving the body clothes, shoes, hair and other details. Offer pictures to use as suggestions. You may have pictures of police officers, superheroes, cartoon characters and so on. When the bodies are finished, have each child stand behind his or her panel and place his or her face into the head hole, while the other kids enjoy the new look. Take lots of photos!

Ages 8–14

Screen Test Party

The stars will shine bright for your Screen Test Party. Give your actors a script and a costume and watch them light up the stage. Set up the lights, turn on the camera and you'll have plenty of action.

Invitations

- Cut out star shapes from silver cardboard and write the party details on the backs. Mail to guests in envelopes filled with confetti stars and covered with star stickers.

- Photocopy a picture of each guest, have the pictures enlarged, cut them into star shapes and write the party details on the backs.

- Take pictures of a completed party invitation and develop into negatives. Cut up the strip of negatives into individual clips and place a clip into each envelope. Have each guest develop the negative into a picture to read the invitation.

Hollywood Star Cake

- Bake two square cakes; cool.
- Cut off all four corners on one of the cakes.

- Place the corners at the sides of the other cake to form a star.
- Ice the cake.
- Serve ice cream bonbons with each slice.

Helpful Hints
- Give the kids costume accessories to enhance their outfits and help them get into their roles more easily.
- Try to have equal parts for all the performers, so everyone is a 'star'.

Prizes and Party Bags

- Send the kids home with Polaroid snapshots of themselves acting out their scenes.
- Hand out plastic sunglasses, movie posters or star magazines.

Costumes

- Ask the guests to come dressed as favourite stars.
- Assign the kids particular stars, to match the script you'll provide.
- Provide sunglasses for each star.

Decorations

- Set the stage for a screen test. Create a platform on which the kids can perform and cover the platform with flooring or carpeting. Hang a drape behind the platform to create a stage. Add paper signs to give the atmosphere of a sound stage. Write such phrases as 'Quiet on the set' and 'Do not enter when camera light is on'.
- Play movie tunes for background music.

Games

306 Get popular movie scripts from the Internet, your local library or a university theatre department. Pull out excerpts and have the kids take turns reading the lines. Have the other guests try to name the movie and the actor who originally said the lines.

307 Have the kids silently act out favourite movie scenes. See if the other guests can identify the scenes.

308 Play a game of Charades, acting out only movie titles.

Ages 10–14

'60s Hippie Party

Put on a tie-dyed T-shirt and pair of bell-bottoms for a trip back to the '60s!

Invitations

- Buy large round coffee filters and a variety of food colourings.
- Dot different colours of food colouring on a coffee filter; the colours will spread and overlap. Allow to dry.
- Write party details on the filter.

- Twist the centre of the filter into a stem and wrap a pipe cleaner around it.
- Fluff the filter's edges to make petals.
- Mail in an envelope decorated with a happy face, a peace symbol and flower stickers.

Vegetarian Pizza

- Buy a pizza base.
- Arrange tomato sauce and vegetables into a peace symbol.
- Bake and serve to waiting hippies.

Prizes and Party Bags

- Tie-dyed pillowcases or T-shirts
- Headbands
- Flower crowns
- Bead necklaces
- '60s music, such as the Beatles or the Monkees
- Candles

Costumes

- Ask the guests to wear bell-bottoms, tie-dyed T-shirts, beads, flower necklaces, long-haired wigs, hats, sandals and so on. Provide accessories from a second-hand shop (or from your cupboard!). Ask each guest to bring a white or pale-coloured pillowcase, or provide one for each of them.

Decorations

- Set out lava lamps.
- String coloured lights around the room.
- Use coloured light globes.
- Fill vases, flowerpots, jars, mugs and so on with big paper flowers.
- Tape peace symbols and '60s posters to the walls.
- Play '60s music.
- Burn incense.
- Light lots of candles and place them all around the room.

Games

309 Gather CDs or cassettes of '60s dance music. Teach the players some dances from that era, such as the Stomp, the Swim and the Mashed Potato. Hold dance contests to see which players can dance each dance the best and award prizes to those players.

310 Buy face paints from a toy or craft store. Let the guests paint flowers and peace symbols on each other's faces. Award a prize for the most creative face.

311 Collect lots of real or artificial flowers. Buy a large needle for each guest and strong thread. Let the guests string the flowers together with the thread to make flower crowns. Have them wear the crowns for the rest of the night.

312 Buy dyes and prepare them according to packet directions. Have guests tie knots in their white or pale-coloured pillowcases and dip the knots in the dyes. Have them untie the knots, tie new ones and dip the new knots in different colours. When everyone is finished dyeing, have them untie all the knots and dry the pillowcases. Let the guests show off the results!

Ages 10–14

Drama and Dreams

This party is all about putting on a play—
from designing a set to developing characters
to staging the performance. Most of the
games and activities are parts of a single play
production. All you need is a short script,
a few actors and some simple materials. Then raise
the curtain on your theatre party!

Invitations

- Fold the short sides of a sheet of A4 paper in to
  meet in the centre.
- Open the folded flaps and write the party details
  inside.
- Close the flaps and seal them shut with a sticker.
- Decorate the front of the flaps to look like theatre
  curtains.

Intermission Bonbon Cake

- Scoop vanilla ice cream into a round bowl.
- Turn bowl upside down onto a serving dish.
- Top with chocolate syrup that hardens when it gets cold.
- Serve giant bonbon cake to kids.

Prizes and Party Bags

- Costume accessories and props
- Scripts for short plays
- Books on acting
- Behind-the-scenes books on theatre

Costumes

- Ask the actors to bring any costumes or accessories they might have, such as wigs, jewellery, gloves, vests, fancy shoes, gowns, hats and so on, to share with the theatre company.

Decorations

- Provide wooden boards so the actors can put together their own stage.
- Give the kids old sheets to make a curtain.
- Have some large sheets of cardboard or cardboard boxes handy for backdrops and props.
- Set up chairs for the audience.
- Set up a video camera to tape the play.
- Hang playbills and theatre posters on the walls.

Games

313 Choose a short script that will fit the actors' abilities and interests. Write brief character descriptions on index cards and place them facedown in a pile. Have one actor draw a card and act out his or her interpretation of the character. If the rest of the group can guess the character, the player who drew that card gets to be that character. If not, they must return the card to the middle of the pile and wait until it's their turn to audition again. Players take turns until all the roles are filled.

314 Have the actors read their parts to get familiar with their characters. Offer costumes and props. Gather the cast for a first reading. After reading through the play once, do a dress rehearsal, running through the play in full costume. If the actors can't memorise their lines, they can disguise their scripts behind magazines or other items. It's showtime! Set up the video camera, invite the audience (family and non-participating guests) and put on your play.

315 (This activity is an alternative to using an existing script.) Divide the group into three or four teams. Tell the actors the theme of the play, such as 'mystery', and the list of characters, such as Detective, Mother, Father, Teenager, Principal, Science Teacher and so on. Assign a character to each actor. Assign each team to write one part of the play. For example, for a mystery play, give Team 1 the introduction of the suspects; Team 2, the opening murder scene; Team 3, the introduction of the detective and interrogation of the suspects; Team 4, the revelation of the killer as the mystery is solved. Let the teams separate to write their portions, so they don't know exactly what the others are writing. Have them write detailed scripts, with dialogue, stage directions and character descriptions. Bring the teams together and have everyone pass out scripts. Beginning with Team 1's first act, perform the play by reading from the scripts and doing the actions as directed. Continue, team by team, to the surprising conclusion.

Ages 10–16

Dinner and Drama Party

Treat the kids to a formal affair with a Dinner and Drama Party. Pick out a play, musical or show that the kids will want to see, then offer a before- or after-dinner party to complete the festivities!

Invitations

- Send formal invitations—engraved, computer-generated, or hand-written using gold ink on white paper or silver ink on black paper. As part of the party information explain that the party will include dinner and a show. Mail the cards in double envelopes to make them look even more impressive.

- Include some home-made theatre tickets or photocopies of original tickets inside the envelope.

- Create a fancy dinner menu and include the party details alongside the food choices. Mail menus in large envelopes.

Helpful Hints
- This party can get expensive, so keep the number of kids to a minimum.
- Choose matinees or lunches for your dinner and drama experience.

Fancy Mini Cakes

- Make mini cakes by cutting a cake into squares and freezing the cakes for easy handling.
- Cover the kids with aprons or smocks to protect their fancy clothes.
- Let the kids decorate their own fancy mini cakes using a piping bag and decorations.
- Before serving, place the decorated mini cakes in the centre of the table for an eye-catching centrepiece!

Prizes and Party Bags

- Give the kids movie coupons and tins of popcorn.
- Hand out playbills, posters of movie stars, T-shirts related to the play or books on which the movie or play was based.

Costumes

- Ask the kids to dress in formal attire—suits, party dresses and so on.
- Have the kids dress in black and white only, and make the party a black-and-white formal affair.
- When the kids arrive, pin real or artificial corsages or boutonnieres on their outfits, offer imitation tiaras or top hats, or provide inexpensive white cotton gloves. These items are usually available at second-hand shops.

Decorations

- Fix up the party room to look like a theatre foyer, with theatre posters of 'Cats', 'Grease', 'Guys and Dolls' and other popular shows decorating the walls.
- Dress up the room by tacking up holiday lights along the ceiling.
- Play show tunes for background music.
- Block off the dining area with sheets or blankets to give the room a feeling of intimacy. Then set the table with your best tablecloth and dishes, and have adult friends serve as waiters.

Games

316 Play word games at the table during your pre- or post-theatre dinner. Write down phrases from popular shows or movies and have the kids guess the play or film titles.

317 Hand out descriptions of special scenes from favourite shows and have the kids act out the scenes for the rest to guess.

318 Play segments of popular songs from movies or shows and have the kids guess the titles.

319 Have the kids make their own tiaras using plastic headbands as foundations. Let them use a glue gun to attach stiff cardboard in gold or silver around the rim. Let the kids decorate the tiaras with sequins, glitter, beads and other baubles.

320 Provide the kids with plain, inexpensive sunglasses, and let them create fancy, Hollywood-style glasses using glitter, rhinestones and puff paints.

Music Parties

These parties are perfect for kids who like to make music, sing and get down on the dance floor!

Ages 3–12

Music Maker Party

There's music in the air when you host a
Music Maker Party—and you don't even
have to carry a tune! Provide the young
musicians with musical opportunities and
watch the party turn up the volume!

Invitations

- Set your invitation to music. Use a portable cassette
  player to record a tune from your own one-kid
  band. Sing the party details as lyrics and mail
  cassettes in padded envelopes.

- Write party details on sheet music and mail to
  guests.

- If you have a friend who likes to sing, hire him or
  her to deliver 'Singing Invitations' right to your
  guests' doorsteps!

Drum Cake

- Bake two round cakes; cool.

- Decorate one layer with chocolate icing, place
  another layer on top, and cover with chocolate icing.

- Decorate the sides with a piping bag, making
  crisscross designs to look like the sides of the drum.

- Top the drum cake with small kazoos, harmonicas or lots of silver bells.

Prizes and Party Bags

- Let the kids take home the musical instruments they make.

- Give the kids song books so they can learn new tunes at home.

- Hand out inexpensive harmonicas, kazoos, noisemakers, whistles or other music-makers.

- Buy small music-box inserts at a fabric or hobby store and drop them into the kids' pockets. Then press their pockets and listen to the surprise music!

Variations

- Take the kids to a concert. Try rock, country or classical music that appeals to kids and let them enjoy the world of music.

- Have a guitar player come to the party to teach the kids how to play a few chords.

Helpful Hint

- If you have valuable musical instruments at the party, be sure to teach the kids how to handle and respect them, or keep the instruments off limits to avoid damage.

Costumes

- Have the kids come dressed as musical instruments (tell them to use their imaginations).

- Ask the kids to come dressed as favourite musicians.

Decorations

- Cut out music notes from black paper and hang them from the ceiling or tape them to the walls.

- Use musical instruments as table centrepieces, and use sheet music as place mats.

- Play a variety of music in the background when you're not performing your own musical entertainment.

Games

321 Play Musical Chairs in a whole new way! Set up chairs in a circle, enough for all but one of the guests. Give each child a kazoo or inexpensive toy horn. Begin the game by playing the kazoo as all the guests walk around the chairs. Stop playing whenever you want. When the playing stops, all players must scramble for a chair. The player who does not find a seat gets to play the kazoo for the others. Continue until only one player remains.

322 Play Instrument Identification. Have musicians play their instruments one at a time for your cassette recorder, or tape-record a variety of instruments from your own music collection. Pause between tunes, and let the kids try to guess what instrument was played.

323 Make your own instruments. Get a book from the library on making simple musical instruments for kids. Make an oatmeal drum, a pie-pan tambourine, an elastic bracelet with bells sewn on, two-pot-lid cymbals, sandpaper wood blocks, toilet-paper kazoos, rice-and-bottle maracas and so on. When the instruments are finished, line the kids up for a concert or march them around the block for a musical parade. Be sure to videotape the concert for playback later.

324 Put on finger plays set to music when you finish making your instruments. Have the kids decorate their fingertips with felt-tip pens to make small people or animal. Then tell the kids to make their 'puppets' dance to the music.

325 Serve food that makes noise! To create a musical meal, try crunchy celery and carrot sticks, cheese and cracker sandwiches, apple-walnut fruit salad, soft drinks or milk shakes with straws and lots of popcorn. Then take turns 'playing' the food to make a meal band!

Ages 6–14

Karaoke Party

Grab the microphone and gather the guests for a sing-along Karaoke Party! Kids love to perform their favourite songs, so let them become the next Madonna, Elvis or Barney for a few musical hours!

Invitations

- Sing your invitation! Buy some inexpensive blank cassettes. Write your lyrics—the party invitation—then sing them into a microphone accompanied by background music. Copy the tape for your guests and mail in padded envelopes.
- If you can't carry a tune, write the party details on blank sheets of music paper and mail to guests.

Sheet Music Cake

- Bake a cake; cool.
- Decorate the cake with white icing.
- Make score lines using chocolate piping bags.
- Create music notes with chocolate chips.

Prizes and Party Bags

- Give the kids song tapes and sheets of song lyrics so they can sing their own tunes at home.
- Hand out copies of the karaoke tapes made at the party.

Variation

- Go to a karaoke restaurant that allows children and let the kids put on their own show. Call ahead to arrange the time and songs.

Helpful Hints

- Write song lyrics in large print for young kids.
- Choose songs that are popular with kids today.
- Let the kids do songs together if they are shy about performing alone.

Costumes

- Have the kids dress as their favourite pop or rock singers so they're ready for the stage!
- Suggest a musical style, such as a '50s or '60s singer, a hip-hop singer or a country or kiddy singer.

Decorations

- Decorate the party room with posters of favourite musical artists.
- Get out your CDs, cassette tapes and records and spread them around the room for inspiration.
- Cut out music notes from black or coloured paper and hang them from the ceiling and on the walls.
- Cover the table with a white sheet of paper, draw score lines to make it look like giant sheet music, then add music notes.
- Write lyrics from favourite songs on sheets of white paper and use them as place mats.

- Set up a stage so your young performers can sing their stuff. To complete the look, add lighting, a curtain and chairs for the audience.

Games

326 Name That Tune: Have the kids guess the song performed by each singer.

327 Name That Tune Version Two: Turning the radio dial and guess the singers and songs.

328 Play karaoke tunes without the lyrics and try to guess the songs.

329 Play You're Next! Have the kids sit in a circle. Start the karaoke music and choose one player to begin. Hand him or her the lyrics to the song and have him or her sing for a minute or so. Then suddenly pass the words to another (unsuspecting) player who must take over the song. Continue until the song is over and everyone has had a turn.

330 Divide the guests into teams and have them create their own lyrics to popular songs. Then have the teams perform the new songs to one another.

331 Teach the kids a song in sign language and have them perform it as a group.

Ages 8–16

DJ Dance Party

Hey, kids! It's All-Dance Radio bringing
you the latest in rap, hip-hop, rock and roll,
punk, new-wave, country and soul! You
choose the music style and the party will
keep the beat!

Invitations

- Write the party details on sheet music (made to
  looks like song lyrics), add a few notes and mail
  your party song to guests.

- Make your own invitation cassette tape by having a
  DJ announce the party information, or impersonate
  a DJ yourself. Set the party talk against a
  background of dance music. Then mail the cassette
  tapes to all your guests.

- Select a time period or style of music and play only
  hits from that era or style, such as '60s music or
  hip-hop songs.

Musical Cake

- To make the cake look like a giant CD or album,
  bake the cake mixture in a round pan.

- Decorate the cake with white icing for a CD and chocolate icing for an album.
- Write song titles and names of groups on top of the cake using piping bags, or make up new groups using the guest-of-honour's name.

Prizes and Party Bags

- Send the rockers home with CD singles.
- Give the kids posters of rock stars.
- Be creative and give out other music-related items, such as harmonicas, music note paper or books about favourite rock stars.

Costumes

- Have the kids dress in dance costumes from different musical eras.
- Have the kids wear fancy socks to the party for dancing and make them remove their shoes when they arrive.

Variations
- Hire a professional or teenager to give the kids dance lessons for the latest steps.
- Take your guests to a rock concert that's appropriate for the kids' ages.

Helpful Hints
- Provide a variety of music, rather than just one kind, so everyone will enjoy the party.
- Clear off an area in the house or garage for dancing and provide chairs and benches for resting between dances.

Decorations

- Cut out music notes from black paper and hang them on the walls and from the ceiling.
- Cover the walls and doors with album and CD covers and posters of favourite rock singers and groups.
- Rent a jukebox (if you can afford it) and ask the supplier to fill it with your favourite hits.
- Hire a professional or amateur DJ to keep the music coming.

Games

332 Have a Copy Me Dance. Select one person as the leader. Every time the leader changes to a new dance style, everyone must follow along until someone else is tagged to take over the lead.

333 Have a dance contest and award prizes for a number of categories, such as the wildest, weirdest, fastest or most entertaining.

334 Offer radio station giveaways. Every so often, stop the music, call out a music trivia question and have the audience guess the answer. Whoever answers first gets a musical prize, such as a picture of a rock star.

Karaoke Celebration

Karaoke is the latest rage. Everyone gets a chance to sing her favourite songs, and off-key singing is welcome!

Invitations

- Write a rough draft of your invitation.
- Sing the party details, setting the words to an instrumental version of a popular song.
- Tape-record your karaoke invitation onto a blank cassette.
- Make a copy for each guest.
- Mail or hand-deliver in padded envelopes.

288

Sheet Music

- Write the party details on a blank page of sheet music between the treble and bass staffs.
- Add musical notes in the staffs to make the words look like song lyrics. For added fun make the words rhyme.
- Photocopy the invitation for each guest and mail.

Microphone Cake

- Bake a cake; cool.
- Cut into the shape of a microphone.
- Decorate with chocolate icing (for top of mike) and white icing (for handle).
- Sprinkle chocolate sprinkles on top of microphone and serve to kids.

Prizes and Party Bags

- Cassettes of each singer's recorded performance
- CD singles of popular songs
- Sheet music of popular songs
- Mini-microphones or megaphones

Costumes

- Ask the singers to wear costumes for their singing debuts.

Decorations

- Make a stage out of a piece of plywood or by spreading a blanket on the floor.
- Place a microphone with stand in the centre of the stage.
- Set up chairs or if it's a slumber party spread sleeping bags for the audience.
- Tape posters of pop stars to the walls.
- Provide costume accessories.

Games

335 Tape-record the first few bars of ten to 12 popular karaoke songs onto a cassette, one right after the other. Select a singer to come on stage. Tell the singer he or she must sing along to the music and keep up as it changes from song to song—without help from the lyrics! If the singer makes a mistake or doesn't keep up, stop the cassette and have someone else try. The player who sings the longest wins a prize.

336 Gather lyrics from a number of popular songs and slowly read them in a monotone voice. The first player to correctly identify the title of the song wins a point. Keep playing until all the lyrics are read. The player with the most points wins a prize.

337 Select a singer to come on stage. Hand them the lyrics to one song, but play an instrumental version of another song. The singer must try to sing the lyrics to fit the music. Have the players vote who did the best job, and that singer wins a prize.

338 Select a singer to come on stage. Give them the lyrics to a popular song. The singer should then rap the words instead of singing them. Have the audience guess the title of the song.

339 Divide the group into teams. Place each team in a separate room with a cassette player and an instrumental version of a popular song. Have the teams make up new lyrics to go with the music—the funnier the lyrics, the better. Once all the teams are ready, regroup and have them take turns singing their made-up tunes.

340 Divide the group into teams. Place each team in a separate room and have them make up a funny rap. Once all the teams are ready, regroup and have them take turns performing their raps.

341 Buy a white T-shirt for each singer. Have the singers create a group design. Provide fabric paints and pens so the singers can draw the design on their T-shirts. Let the singers wear the T-shirts for a group karaoke song and videotape the performance.

342 Have everyone pair up except one player. Turn on the music and let the pairs dance. After a few moments, the extra player must tag someone and take their place in the dance. The tagged dancer must tag someone else and take their place. Tagging continues until someone tags a player who has already been tagged. The tagger is then out of the game.

343 Choose one guest to be the DJ and have the other guests pair up. The DJ starts the music and the pairs begin dancing. When the DJ stops the music he or she must join the dance and everyone must find a new partner. The player who doesn't find a partner becomes the DJ. Continue playing until everyone has had a chance to be the DJ.

344 Buy a pair of colourful socks for each guest. Lay socks flat on a piece of cardboard and trace around each sock, making the tracing a little larger than the sock. Cut out the tracings and insert them into the socks. Offer guests a variety of puff paints or fabric paints and let them paint creative designs on the socks. If it's a sleepover, let the socks dry overnight, then give them to the guests.

Camping and Scavenger Parties

These parties are great for some backyard
exploration and excitement!

Ages 5–10

Cool Camp-in

You don't have to wait for summer to go camping; you can have a Cool Camp-in any time of the year!

Skylight card

- Buy black paper and glow-in-the-dark stickers and pens.
- Fold black paper in half.
- Attach glow-in-the-dark stars to the front of the card.
- Inside, write the party details with glow-in-the-dark pens.
- Tuck the invitation in a padded envelope along with a miniature torch.
- Instruct guests to shine the torches on the cards (inside and out), then turn off the lights to see the surprise.

Marshmallow Mini Cakes

- Heat marshmallows in microwave to soften them.
- Give the kids giant biscuits.
- Get the kids to put warm marshmallows on two biscuits and squash them together for a gooey treat.

Prizes and Party Bags

- Torches
- Glow-in-the-dark pens, stars, necklaces and trinkets
- Camping gear
- Stuffed animals
- Scout camping handbooks

- Ask the campers to bring their own sleeping bags and any camping equipment they want to share, such as torches, tents, mess kits and so on. Have them bring their favourite stuffed animals, too.

Decorations

- Stick glow-in-the-dark stars all over the walls and ceiling, so when the lights go out, the stars will shine.
- Spread sleeping bags on the floor. For makeshift tents, string ropes across the room and hang blankets over them.
- Spread a picnic tablecloth on the floor.
- Make a campfire: Cut orange cellophane into long strips and tie them to logs. Set the logs in the middle of the room and place a small electric fan nearby to make the cellophane whip around like flames.
- Place small mats around the campfire.
- Play recordings of animals, rivers, waterfalls or other nature sounds in the background.
- Place stuffed animals behind the furniture as if they are hiding in the forest.

Games

345 Write the names of many different animals on slips of paper and place them in a container. Hang a sheet across one end of the room and point a light at the back of the sheet. Have the kids sit on the other side. One player must draw a slip from the container, then stand behind the sheet in front of the light and act out the animal. The audience must watch the shadow play and guess the animal. Give a point for each correct guess and then award a prize to the guest with the most points.

346 On slips of paper, write a number of creepy sounds like a squeaky door, rattling chain, rustling mouse, moaning ghost, rolling thunder, creaking staircase and so on. Have everyone sit in a circle in near-darkness. One player must choose a paper and recreate the creepy sound using only their voice. The player who first guesses the correct answer wins a point.

347 Gather round the campfire and sing camp songs. Sing in rounds, make up new songs and change the words in old favourites like 'Row, Row, Row Your Boat' and 'Twinkle, Twinkle, Little Star'.

348 Go to the library and check out some books on ghost stories. Memorise and recite the stories or read them at the campfire. Take turns telling ghost stories and urban legends.

Ages 6–14

Camp-out Party

Host an all-nighter in your own backyard camp ground and watch the happy campers enjoy the great outdoors! Pitch the tent, turn on the torches, cook the marshmallows, then hit the sack!

Invitations

- Send the guests a package of freeze-dried food or ice cream that expert campers use (available at sporting goods and nature stores). Write the party details on the outside of the package using permanent felt-tip pen, or tape the invitation to the food packet.
- Send the campers a compass with a sheet of directions to the party, to help them find their way.

Camping Cake

- Bake a cake; cool.
- Decorate with a favourite icing.
- Top the cake with natural snack items such as coconut, seeds, chopped nuts, cereal bits, sultanas and chopped dried fruit.

Prizes and Party Bags

- Send the campers home with brand-new comic books.

- Give each kid a compass to take home.

- Give the kids packets of ice cream or other freeze-dried treats to take home.

- Hand out miniature torches or other inexpensive camping gear.

Variation

- Take the kids to real camping grounds and have your party in the wilderness! Ask the kids to bring their camping gear, then pitch the tents and hike around the grounds. Be sure to invite a couple of extra parents to help out for safety's sake.

Helpful Hints

- Some kids may be scared of the dark, so have night-lights available outside.

- Consider inviting a couple of parents to join the overnighter, for those kids who need the extra security of mum or dad.

- When walking around at night, have plenty of torches, move slowly, and don't go into poorly lit areas.

Costumes

- Have the kids come to the party dressed for camping in the wilderness, wearing hiking boots, camp shirts, shorts or jeans and hats.

Decorations

- Decorate the tent with streamers, balloons and funny signs.

- If you don't have a tent, fold a large blanket or tarp over a clothes line or hang a piece of rope between two trees to make your own tent.

- Have a supply of backpacks, sleeping bags, camping gear, comic books and other camping-related items. (You may want to ask the kids to bring some of their own camping gear to supplement your supply.)
- To add to the atmosphere of a back yard forest, paint glow-in-the-dark eyes on paper, cut them out and staple them around the yard—on bushes, to the fence, on the trees—so it looks like wild animals are keeping an 'eye' on the campers in the darkness.
- If you have any tapes of animal sounds, play them when the kids go to bed.

Games

349 Play Trapped in the Sleeping Bag. Have two kids get inside one sleeping bag, then zip it all the way up the sides, making sure both players have their hands down at their sides. Tell them you hear a croc coming down the path and they have only a few seconds to get out of the sleeping bag, so they'd better move fast! Time the campers to see how long it takes them to get out of the sleeping bag. Then try the game again with another couple of kids and compare escape times.

350 Have a sleeping-bag sack race. Have everyone hop inside their sleeping bags from the start to the finish line.

351 Get out the torches and take a midnight walk around the neighborhood, under the leadership of an adult.

352 Have one group walk around the backyard, leaving clues as they go, such as arrows made from lined-up rocks or a trail of bread crumbs. Then have a second group follow the clues left by the first group.

353 Have the kids sit in a circle and share ghost stories.

Ages 7–10

Hide 'n' Hunt

All kids love treasure hunts—the suspense of the search, the joy of discovery! There are so many variations on this Hide 'n' Hunt party that you can easily come up with your own exciting versions!

Invitations

- Make Treasure Chest invitations by cutting out rectangles from brown paper. Fold each rectangle in half to make a treasure chest. Use a felt-tip pen to draw a chest on the outside of the cards. Write the party details inside, then glue on sequins or glitter.

- Send the guests on a treasure hunt for their invitations! Hide five clues around each guest's front yard, then mail the first clue to begin the hunt. Let the last clue lead the guest to the party invitation.

- Write out the party details on a large sheet of paper. Cut or tear the paper into pieces, taking care to keep the individual words intact. Send one or two words to each guest with a note that the other guests have the rest of the pieces. (Be sure to provide their names and phone numbers.) The guests will have to call each other to get all the words to the invitation, then unscramble them to figure out the party details.

Treasure Chest Cake

- Bake a cake and cover with chocolate icing.

Helpful Hints
- Make sure there is enough treasure for everyone so no one feels left out.

- Decorate the cake pan and set it at a right angle to the cake to look like the open lid of a treasure chest.

- Decorate with piping bags.

- Place chocolate gold coins and lolly jewellery on the cake.

- Send the kids home with surprise balls and chocolate coins.

- Give them books about buried treasures, pirate adventures, archaeological discoveries or famous mysteries.

Costumes

- Ask the guests to wear pirate outfits—eye patches, bandanas, striped shirts and pirate hats.

- Have the kids dress as archaeologists searching for buried treasures of the past.

- Have a mystery hunt and ask the guests to come as a favourite detective.

Decorations

- Find some cardboard gift boxes, spray-paint them gold and set them around the party area as treasure chests. Fill them with chocolate gold coins or inexpensive jewellery from second-hand shops.

- Cover the table with white paper. Draw a treasure map on it using colourful felt-tip pens. Have the map lead the guests to treats or the party cake. Provide different clues to the goodies at each place setting.

Games

354 Buried Treasure Hunt: Hide a number of plastic toys and jewellery in the backyard. Divide the group into teams and give each team a list of poetic clues, such as 'Roses are red, Violets are blue, My garden grows gems, Can you find one or two'. The team that finds the most items wins. Let the kids keep what they find.

355 Following Footsteps: Draw out clues to a special treasure on the back of cut-out footprints. Set the first footprint at the starting line and have the kids read the clue and try to figure out where the next clue is hidden. For added fun, hide two different sets of clues and have the kids search for the treasure as competing teams.

356 Treasure Hunt: Divide the kids into two teams; put one team in the front yard and the other team in the backyard. Give each team paper and a pencil. Have them bury a prize somewhere, then create a map that will lead to the treasure. The teams then switch maps and get to search for the other team's buried treasure.

357 Treasure Surprise Ball: Buy enough different small toys so that each guest will get one. Get a long crepe-paper streamer; wrap the first toy with the streamer until it is shaped like a small ball. Place another toy on the crepe-paper ball and continue to wrap until that toy is also covered. Keep adding toys and wrapping them until all the toys have been included. Tape the end closed. Seat the guests in a circle and play some music while the players pass the ball to each other. When the music stops, the player holding the ball gets to unwrap it slowly until he or she finds a toy. That player is then out of the game. Play until everyone has a toy.

358

Treasure Chests: Have the kids make their own treasure chests. Ask each kid to bring a shoe box to the party. Let them paint the boxes gold, then decorate the boxes with puff paints, felt-tip pens, jewels, sequins, glitter, play coins and other shiny items. The kids can then take the chests home and fill them with their own treasures.

Ages 8–12

Scavenger Hunt

Come for a scavenger hunt and find all sorts of fun, cool goodies!

Invitations

- Make a list of ingredients to make a pizza or another snack.

- For each guest, fold a sheet of light-coloured paper in half.

- On the front of the card, write 'Come to a Scavenger Hunt!'

- Open the card, and on the left side write 'Please bring (one of the pizza or snack ingredients) to the Scavenger Hunt'. Ask them not to tell anyone what they are bringing. When each guest arrives with their ingredient, have them stash it in a paper bag. Use a different paper bag for each guest and label each with the guest's name. Keep the bags hidden from the guests until it's time to use them.
- On the right side, write the party details.
- Tuck the card into an envelope and mail.

Scavenger Cake

- Bake two round cakes; cool.
- Place the cakes on top of each other and hollow out the middle.
- Hide ingredients such as chocolate chips, sultanas, chopped up fruit and sprinkles around the house and have the kids search for them.
- Let the kids fill the cake with ingredients and then ice and serve.

Prizes and Party Bags

- Decorative bags
- Ingredients for a biscuit recipe
- Pads of paper
- Mini torches

- Have the guests bring their pyjamas and sleeping bags.

Decorations

- Make collection boxes: Gather cardboard boxes and decorate them with contact paper or wrapping paper and label each one with a different guest's name.
- Write lists of silly items for scavenger hunts and tape them to the walls. You might list things like a picture of the Invisible Man, a lock of Leonardo DiCaprio's hair, one of the Backstreet Boys, thousand-dollar bill, goat and copy of next week's newspaper.

Games

359 Divide the players into two teams and place each team in a separate room. Give each team pencils and a notepad and have each list ten items for the other team to find. Decide beforehand whether the items are to be found in the neighbourhood or in the house. Read the lists to make sure the items are appropriate. Give each team its scavenger hunt list and a bag for the loot. Tell the teams how much time they have to hunt, then set them hunting! When time is up, count the items each team found. The team with the most items from its list wins a prize.

360 Hide items in the yard for the players to find. List on paper what you hid. When it's dark outside, give a copy of the list and a torch to each player and let them hunt in the dark!

361 For each player, give a copy of the same list of items likely to be found in a teen magazine, such as a photo of a movie star, instructions for a craft or a makeover, picture of a new hairstyle or ads for beauty products, underwear, snack foods, music or upcoming movies. Give each player paper, scissors and a different teen magazine. At the word 'Go' have the players quickly search through the magazines and cut out the items on their lists. When time is up, see which player cut out the most correct items. Award a prize to that player.

362 Have the guests collect three unusual items from designated rooms in the house or from the yard. When everyone finds their items, have them sit in a circle and set the items in the middle. Each guest must take a turn creating a silly story incorporating their collected items.

Ages 8–12

Night Owls

The dark offers a mysterious setting for a Night Owls party, where shadows dance and starlights twinkle. Tell the kids to keep their torch handy—it's time for some night-time fun!

Invitations

- Find pictures of owls or draw your own and cut them out. Write the party details on the backs and mail to the guests.

- Mail tiny torches to the kids in padded envelopes. Write the party details on small cards and tie them to the torches with string.

- Cut out and fold invitations from black paper. Write the party details with a glow-in-the-dark pen. On the outside of the envelopes, tell the guests to hold the card up to a light bulb for a few seconds, then turn off the lights to read the party invitation.

Milky Way Cake

- Bake a cake and decorate with melted Milky Way bars mixed with chocolate icing.

- Make stars and planets using a piping bag of white icing.
- Before serving, place lit mini torches around the cake.

Prizes and Party Bags

- Give the kids decorated socks to wear home.
- Find nightcaps at the novelty store and give them to the kids.
- Let the kids keep the mini torches from the party.

Variation
- Make a trip to the local planetarium or set up a telescope in the yard.

Helpful Hint
- Some kids are afraid of the dark, so make sure everyone has a torch handy.

Costumes

- Have the guests come in pyjamas for your night-time party. Ask them to bring a robe and slippers, too.
- If the kids have their own torches, ask them to bring them along.

Decorations

- Create an outside 'room' by stringing up ropes between trees and fences and hanging sheets and blankets over the ropes to form walls.
- Pitch a tent for the kids to sleep in.
- Arrange the sleeping bags in a circle with the kids' heads toward the centre so they can chat.
- Cut out stars from glow-in-the-dark paper and hang them from the trees.
- Cut out eyes from white paper; paint the eyes with glow-in-the-dark paints. Tape the eyes in pairs around the outdoor area so the kids will think that animals are watching them!
- Play a tape of animal sounds in the background.
- Give the kids mini torches to shine.

Games

363 Blind Touch: Collect a number of items that are interesting to touch, such as a fuzzy slipper, a toothbrush, a sponge, a handful of fake slime and so on. Turn out the lights and pass around the items in the dark. Let the kids feel the items and guess what they are.

364 Midnight Magic: Show the kids how to do simple magic tricks, then let them come up one at a time and perform the tricks. Darkness gives the magic tricks more power!

365 Pillow Fight: Have the guests bring their own pillows to the party, then divide the kids into two teams and have a pillow fight. Place the teams on opposite sides of the yard; the kids then toss the pillows at one another and try to hit someone on the other team. Anyone who is hit is out of the game. The last team standing wins!

366 Blindfold Race: Split the kids into two teams. Blindfold one kid on each team. The teams must yell out directions to their blindfolded teammate as he or she attempts to walk an obstacle course made of soft items like pillows and blankets. Once the blindfolded racer reaches the end, he or she races back and gives another teammate the blindfold. The first team to finish wins.

367 Glow-in-the-Dark Art: Let the kids draw or paint on white paper with glow-in-the-dark pens or paints. When they're finished, turn the lights off and watch the pictures appear!

368 Batman Signals: Let the kids make their own Batman Signals using paper and torches. Have the kids cut out different designs from black paper, making sure each design is a little larger than the lens of their torches. Tape the cut-out design onto the light, then shine the light against a flat surface in the dark. Watch the image appear!

Ages 8–14

Crazy Camp-out

Hosting an overnighter in your own backyard is a great way to entertain the kids. The Crazy Camp-out party provides lots of ideas for night-time fun in your very own make-believe wilderness.

Invitations

- Cut out tent-shaped cards from brown paper with the fold at the top of the tent. Open the front of the tent and write the party details inside. Add a drawing of a kid in a sleeping bag.
- Send the campers a pack of freeze-dried food with the party details written on the back. Mail in small boxes or padded envelopes.

Cake Log

- Bake a cake on a pan that has at least a 3 centimetre edge. Because the cake is very thin, keep an eye on it so it doesn't burn.
- Allow the cake to cool, then decorate it with chocolate icing.
- Sprinkle on chopped nuts, sultanas and seeds.

- Beginning at one end roll the cake lengthwise into a log.
- Ice with more chocolate icing, sprinkle with seeds and nuts and cut into slices.

Variation
- Take the kids camping at a real camping ground.

Helpful Hint
- Sleep outside with the kids to make sure they stay safe and feel secure.

Prizes and Party Bags

- Send the campers home in the morning with mini torches, freeze-dried food, a compass and a fresh selection of comic books.

Costumes

- Ask the campers to come dressed in appropriate camping attire, with hiking boots, hats and a jacket for the cold night air.

- Have the kids bring pyjamas, sleeping bags and other camping equipment to use at the party.

- Ask the guests to bring along any box games or comic books they might wish to share.

Decorations

- Set up a large tent for the campers to sleep in. Borrow a few tents if you need to and make a tent village.

- Paint cardboard with glow-in-the-dark paint, then cut out dozens of eyes. Fill in the centres of the eyes with a black felt-tip pen, then stick pairs of eyes all around the camping area. When night falls, the eyes will glow in the dark.

- Make owls out of paper and prop them on the fence.

- Set out camping equipment on a picnic table. Set the table with bandana place mats, personalised for each camper with puffy paints. Set a mini torch at each place.

- Once night falls, play tapes of nature sounds on a portable cassette player.

Games

369 Torch Tag: When it gets dark, give one player a torch and have that player close his or her eyes and count to 20 while the other players hide. He or she then tries to spot the other players by shining the torch around the yard. Anyone who gets tagged by the light is out of the game. Play until everyone is caught, then select a new player to hold the torch.

370 Name that Noise: Campers always seem to hear funny noises when they're out in the wilderness. For this game, tape-record a bunch of noises, such as a dog barking, a chain rattling, a door creaking, a motor running, an owl hooting and so on. After dark, gather the campers around the fire and play the tape-recorded noises. Stop the tape after each noise and let the kids write down what they think the noise is. Whoever gets the most noises correct wins a prize.

371 The Ghost that Never Dies Story: When it gets dark, have the campers sit around the campfire. Begin a spooky story about a ghost. Stop at an exciting part in the story. Have the next player continue the story, also ending at an exciting part. Continue until everyone has had a chance to add to the story.

372 Midnight Hike: When it gets dark, have everyone hold hands in a long line. Lead the group on a midnight hike around the dark yard. Put up obstacles for the hikers to climb over, around, under or through.

Sand and Water Parties

The kids will love spending time on their own tropical island, or splish-splashing around on a warm party day!

Tropical Island Party

Take the kids to the tropics—right in your own backyard! Slap on the suntan lotion and grab the grass skirts—it's time for some fun in the sun!

Invitations

- Use holiday postcards featuring a tropical beach. Write, 'Wish you were here!' on the photo side of the postcard—then print the party details on the back. Mail to your guests.
- Create your own airline tickets, good for a free trip to your tropical paradise. Write the party details on the ticket to read as destination, time of departure and arrival, and other party information.
- Create a brochure, writing the party information as an advertisement for a tropical paradise.

Tropical Island Cake

- Bake a rectangular cake; cool.
- Cover half the cake with white icing tinted blue, to look like the sea.

- Cover the other half of the cake with white icing and sprinkle brown sugar on top to look like sand.

- Set toy people on the sand and have fish or a tiny shark coming up out of the ocean.

Variations
- Have your party at the beach!
- Invite real hula dancers to entertain the kids.

Helpful Hint
- If you have water at the party be sure to watch over small kids and non-swimmers.

Prizes and Party Bags

- Send the kids home from their tropical holiday with sand toys, sunglasses and beach towels.
- Give the kids grass skirts and hula-hoops.

Costumes

- Ask the guests to come as hula dancers, bathing beauties, surfers or even tourists, complete with loud Hawaiian print shirts, straw hats, sunglasses and cameras.

- When your guests arrive, dress them up with grass skirts made from sheets of crepe paper.

- Ask your guests to bring bathing suits to the party.

Decorations

- Turn your yard into a tropical paradise with crepe paper streamers, torches or holiday lights and big pictures of colourful fish and marine life.
- Hang up posters of tropical islands.
- Decorate the table with postcards of various beaches.
- Make a sandbox and fill it with sand toys.
- Fill a kiddy pool with water for a splash in the 'ocean'.
- Cut out palm trees from large sheets of paper and tack them to the fence.

Games

373 Find Pirate's Treasure. Bury some toys in the sand and let the kids dig them out. When they find a toy, they get to keep it, but they must drop out of the digging and allow other players to find the treasures.

374 Play Musical Pools. Set large pans of water in a circle, enough for all but one player. Play music as the kids, in bathing suits, march around the pools of water. When you stop playing the music, the kids must scramble for a pool and sit down. The player who does not find a pool is out of the game. Remove one pan of water and continue playing until only one player remains.

375 Have a Limbo Contest and see how low they can go. Hold a broomstick or bamboo stick and have the players try to duck under it by bending backwards. Play some music as the line limbos under the limbo stick. After everyone has had a turn going under the stick, lower it and go again. Keep playing until only one player remains. The remaining player gets a prize.

376 Get out a hula hoop and have a contest to see how long each player can keep the hoop in the air. Try this game while wearing grass skirts. Younger kids may have some trouble keeping the hoop in the air for any length of time, so have them jump through the hoops instead.

377 Give the kids coconuts and let them make funny faces out of the coconuts. Point out the two dark circles that form the coconut 'eyes', then give the kids puff paints, regular paints or felt-tip pens to create crazy coconut heads. When they're finished, hammer a large nail into the top of each coconut, insert a straw into each hole and let the kids drink the coconut milk.

Ages 6–12

Splish-splash Party

What's the only ingredient you need for a successful Splish-splash party? Water! Watch the wet ones frolic in the surf and sun. If you don't live near the surf, make your own Water Wonderland right in the backyard. It's time to get wet!

Invitations

- For a fascinating underwater invitation, use a permanent felt-tip pen to write the party details on a piece of colourful plastic, such as a cut-up beach ball or margarine tub lids. Insert the plastic invitation into a sealable lunch bag. Fill the bag half-full with blue-tinted water (use blue food colouring). Add plastic or metallic confetti to make the water sparkle, then glue the bag shut with super glue. Allow to dry, then place in a small box and mail.

Rainbow Cake

- Bake two round cakes; cool.
- Cut the cakes in half cross-wise.
- Place all four halves together to form a large half circle and ice the sides so they stick together.

- Turn the cake onto its flat side, with the rounded side up.

- Divide a batch of white icing into individual bowls, and tint each bowl a different colour—to make the colours of the rainbow.

- Decorate the cake in rows to create a rainbow effect.

Variations
- Have the party at a lake or pool.
- If you have water slides nearby, spend a hot afternoon sliding your way to cool, wet fun.

Helpful Hints
- Make sure everyone knows they're going to get wet at this wild party.
- Have the kids wear sunglasses to protect their eyes.
- Tell all the kids to use sunscreen.

Prizes and Party Bags

- Send the kids home with new towels.
- Hand out squirt guns, water sponges, sand pails, water goggles or fancy sprinkler heads.
- Give the kids bubble solution to take home.

Costumes

- Have the kids come dressed in clothes they don't mind getting wet. Bathing suits are preferred, but it's sometimes fun to get wet in shorts and a T-shirt for a change.
- Ask the kids to bring beach towels, sunscreen, sunglasses and hats.

Decorations

- Host the party outside where the water is plentiful and you don't have to worry about making a mess.
- Cut out blue waves from paper, and tack them to the top of the fence, to give the feeling of being under water.
- Get out the sprinklers with a variety of heads and hoses, the wading pool and any other fun water toys you have around the house.
- Don't forget the squirt guns, water pails and sponges!

Games

378 Have a Water War with squirt guns, wet sponges, and water pails.

379 Create a Splash Machine. Have the kids line up, then pass buckets of water from person to person and dump them into the kiddy pool. Watch the kids get all wet!

380 Throw coins into the pool, and let the kids scramble for them.

381 Have a tug-of-war by the wading pool. Separate the kids into two teams, station them on opposite sides of the pool and have each team try to pull the other team into the water using rope.

382 Make a slippery slide on the lawn. Spread large plastic garbage bags over the grass and attach a hose at one end.

383 Make your own sponges to use in the pool or bath. Give the kids coloured sponges and let them cut the sponges into various shapes. Then let them take the sponges into the water to play, or have the kids use the sponges to paint with tempera paint on large sheets of paper.

384 Fill the kiddy pool with water, and add ⅓ cup of dishwashing liquid and two teaspoons of glycerine; mix well. Twist metal coat hangers or pipe cleaners into shapes and use them to create bubbles from the giant pool of solution. Warn the kids not to splash in the solution, since the soap will sting their eyes.

Ages 6–12

Sand Castle Party

Here's a weather-themed party that's perfect for summer. Or host it in the winter to warm yourselves up.

Invitations

- Cut out yellow suns from paper and write the party details on the suns in a circle. Place the suns in individual sealable sandwich bags and add a little sand for fun.
- Mail postcards of the beach to get your guests in the mood for fun in the sun.

Sunburst Cake

- Bake one round cake and six cupcakes.
- Set the cupcakes around the outside of the round cake to make rays.
- Tint white icing with yellow food colouring and decorate the cakes with yellow icing.
- Give the sun a face using decorator piping bags.

Prizes and Party Bags

- Send the kids home with buckets for the beach and shovels.
- Give the kids their own sunglasses.
- Hand out towels or beach hats.

Variation

- Instead of hosting a sand castle party in the summer, have a make-believe summer party in the winter. Use your imagination to pretend it's cold when it's hot and vice versa.

Helpful Hint

- If the weather won't cooperate, create your own realistic temperature in the party room. For a winter party turn down the heat and turn on the air conditioner. For a summer party turn up the heat and make it toasty inside.

Costumes

- Have the kids wear bathing suits, shorts, tank tops or Hawaiian shirts.
- Provide sunglasses, suntan lotion, beach hats and other sunshine items.

Decorations

- Set up a 'beach' in the back yard by filling the sandbox with beach toys.
- Get the sprinklers going and fill the wading pool for water games and fun.
- Make an ocean by cutting wave shapes out of blue paper and hanging them on the fence. Add tropical fish cut-outs.
- Make a cardboard boat and add lots of beach balls to create a party atmosphere.
- Play Hawaiian music in the background.

Games

385 Have swim races in the backyard pool or nearby lake or beach.

386 Do gymnastics on the lawn.

387 Play Snake in the Grass. Have one player turn the sprinkler on and off, without looking at the rest of the players. Have the other players run through the area where the sprinklers are. The player who first makes it from one end of the area to the other without getting sprayed wins.

388 Make sand candles. Dig a hole in the sandbox, pour in wax, add a wick and pull out a sand candle. Candle wax and wicks are available at craft and hobby stores.

Ages 7–12

Cool in the Pool

For a hot time in the summer sun, host a Cool in the Pool party. All you need to do is lather on the sun block—the water will entertain the kids for hours. Just keep the towels handy for the soaking finale!

Invitations

- Send the swimmers postcards of hotel swimming pools, beaches or other water resorts with party details on the back.

- Buy some inexpensive sunglasses and decorate them with puff paint pens. Attach cards with party details. Mail to guests in small boxes.

- Pour a little water into small plastic containers, tint blue and seal the lids shut with super glue. Write the party details on the containers with a felt-tip pen. Mail to guests in small boxes.

Pool Party Cake

- Bake a cake and decorate with white icing.
- Tint some of the white icing blue. Decorate the

centre of the cake to make the pool.

- Tint shredded coconut green with food colouring and sprinkle around the outside of the pool to make grass.
- Insert plastic sharks in the pool for decoration.

Prizes and Party Bags

- Send the guests home with an inflatable pool toy, such as an inner tube or air mattress.
- Give the kids sunglasses to take home.
- Buy inexpensive beach towels and give one to each guest.
- Offer lunch bags filled with lolly fish.

Costumes

- Have the kids wear their bathing suits. Ask them to

also bring towels, cover-ups and a change of clothes.

Decorations

- Drape fishnets along the fence and attach plastic fish as if they have been caught.

Variation
- Take the kids to the beach or a local community pool for the party.

Helpful Hint
- Be sure all the kids can swim. Never leave the pool area unattended.

- Set water toys around the party area and place a rubber duck on the table as a centrepiece.

- Fill the pool with inner tubes, beach balls and other floating toys.

- Hang posters of tropical vacations on the fence or along the side of the house.

- Play Hawaiian or Beach Boys music in the background.

Games

389 Super Marco Polo: To play the traditional version of Marco Polo, swimmers move around the pool while the player chosen as Marco Polo tries to find them with his or her eyes closed. When he or she calls out 'Marco', the other swimmers must respond with 'Polo'. With Super Marco Polo, no one says anything and ALL the swimmers must close their eyes! When Marco Polo catches a swimmer, the swimmer switches places with Marco.

390 Escape from Jaws: One swimmer is chosen to play the shark and the rest of the swimmers must try to keep from being eaten by 'Jaws' as they swim around the pool. Whoever the shark touches is out; play until only one swimmer remains.

391 Gold Diggers: Paint small rocks with gold paint. When dry, drop them onto the bottom of the pool. Have the swimmers stand around the pool. On the word 'Go' they all jump into the pool and try to retrieve as many gold nuggets as they can. The one with the most nuggets wins a prize.

392 Rescue Rope: Toss some items that float into the pool, such as a chunk of wood, an inflated toy and so on. Give one player a length of rope and have him or her try to lasso an item and bring it safely to shore. For a competition, give all the players a rope and have them race to bring their items to shore.

393 Water Basketball: Buy a water basketball hoop or make your own using a small ring of plastic—a little larger than the ball—that will float in the pool. Divide the players into two teams and have them play basketball in the water. Another option is to play volleyball by stringing a net or rope across the pool.

394 Ocean in a Bottle: Give each guest an empty clear plastic water bottle. Have them fill the bottle three-quarters full with water, add several drops of food colour, some glitter and fill it the rest of the way with cooking oil. Seal the lid shut with Super Glue and let the kids enjoy their Ocean in a Bottle.

395 Give the kids watercolours and paper and let them paint a beach scene.

Party Island

Spend the night shipwrecked on a deserted island with no hope of rescue until morning!

Invitations

- Ask your local travel agent for brochures or booklets on tropical holidays.
- Cut out tropical pictures and glue each onto one side of an index card to make a postcard.
- Pour a cup of salt into a bowl.

- Rub the salt with a large stick of yellow chalk to make 'sand'.
- Brush a line of glue along the bottom of the post card and sprinkle with the salt.
- Turn the card over and draw a vertical line down the middle. Then write the party details on the left side and the guest's name and address on the right side.
- Tuck the card in a stamped, addressed envelope along with a small paper umbrella; mail.

Ice Cream Island Cakes

- Pour a small amount of blueberry sauce into a bowl.
- Scoop a ball of ice cream and roll it in green-tinted coconut.
- Drop the coconut-covered ice cream ball in the centre of the blueberry sauce.
- Add a paper umbrella to the ice cream island. Serve one island to each guest.

Prizes and Party Bags

- Sunglasses
- Anklets
- Sailor hats and straw hats
- Goldfish biscuits and lolly fish

Costumes

- Have the castaways dress in shorts and summer shirts and encourage them to go barefoot when they arrive. Ask them to bring large beach towels. Give each a sailor hat or a straw hat, a flower lei and a grass skirt.

Decorations

- Spread sleeping bags on the floor and cover them with beach towels.

- String coloured lights from the ceiling.

- Stick glow-in-the-dark stars on the ceiling so the guests can sleep under the stars.

- Cut tree trunks from brown paper and large palm leaves from green paper. Tape the palm trees to the walls.

- Use coconuts as place markers. Serve beverages in hollow coconut halves garnished with paper umbrellas.

- Carve a pineapple boat for a centrepiece.

- Play Hawaiian, calypso or reggae music in the background.

Games

396 Have two players hold a long stick or pole horizontally, about a metre above the ground. Line up the rest of the players and turn on some calypso music. Have the players try to walk under the limbo stick by bending their knees and arching their backs. After everyone has a turn, lower the limbo stick and repeat. Keep playing until the limbo stick is so low, only one person can go under it. As a fun variation, play in the dark with a torch instead of a limbo stick!

397 Cut large circular 'stones' from paper. Place a stone at one end of the room. Place another stone 30 centimetres away from the first. Continue setting down stones, increasing the distance between them. One at a time, have the players start at the first stone and try to follow the stones to safety. A player who can't reach a stepping stone sinks in the ocean and is out of the game. The player to make it to the farthest stepping stone wins a prize.

398 Inflate a beach ball. Have the players sit in a circle. Tell a player to toss the ball to anyone in the circle, who must volley it immediately to another player. Keep the ball in the air and moving fast—no holding it even for a second. Any player who misses the ball is out of the game.

399 Buy crepe paper in a variety of colours, one package per guest. Hand out the crepe paper and have the guests unwrap their packages. Wrap the paper around each guest's waist and pin or tape it closed. Have the guests take turns cutting each other's skirts into dangling strips. Do a hula dance when the grass skirts are ready.

400 At a craft store buy artificial flowers, colourful string and large needles. Measure and cut enough lengths of string to make one lei for each guest. Have guests thread flowers onto the string to make floral leis. Or make lolly leis by tying wrapped lollies together with colourful ribbons.

401 Buy an inexpensive pair of sunglasses for each guest. Let guests decorate their glasses with puff paints, glitter, stickers, ribbons and other items.

402 At a bead or craft store, buy a variety of beads, some elastic string and needles. Measure and cut enough lengths of elastic string to make an anklet for each guest. Set out the beads, strings and needles and let the guests make their own anklets. Help the guest tie their anklets around their ankles.

Ages 8–12

Beach Party

Put on your bathing suits, bring your towels and head on over for a Beach Party. No need to fly to the islands—you can turn your backyard into a tropical paradise with a little imagination and creativity!

Invitations

- Buy some coconuts and write the party details right on them with a black felt-tip pen. For fun, make a funny face on the coconut first. Hand deliver or mail to guests.

- Make paper coconuts by folding sheets of brown paper in half and cutting circles. Do not cut where the paper is folded; this will hold the two parts of the card together. Use a felt pen to add coconut details and a funny face. Place in envelopes with a little bit of sand and tiny, inexpensive shell necklaces. Mail to guests.

- Collect brochures of the tropics from travel agencies and write party details inside, then mail to guests.

Pineapple Upside-down Cake

- Mix cake according to directions.
- Layer pineapple slices in the bottom of a sheet cake pan, fill holes with maraschino cherries and pour in the liquid of canned pineapples.
- Pour in the cake batter and bake according to package directions.
- When done flip the cake over onto platter—pineapple side up.
- Top with tiny paper umbrellas for decoration.

Prizes and Party Bags

- Give the kids shell necklaces and lolly necklaces to wear home.
- Let the guests have their own beach balls.
- Offer everyone a beach kit filled with sunscreen, inexpensive sunglasses, a water bottle and a fan.

Costumes

- Ask the vacationers to come dressed as tourists in Hawaiian shirts and hula skirts or ask them to wear their bathing suits under regular clothes.

Variations
- Take the kids to the local beach and enjoy your party on real sand.
- Turn the event into a pool party.

Helpful Hint
- Be sure to cover everyone with sunscreen protection lotion before they get too much sun.

Decorations

- Drape fishnets over the fence and the party table to create a tropical look.

- Hang plastic fish from the fence or the trees. Place extra fish on the table, personalised with each guest's name.

- String up coloured lights if the party is at night.

- Fill the party area with large paper flowers and lots of tropical fruit, such as coconuts, bananas and pineapples.
- If you have a surfboard, it makes a great prop.
- Hang tiny shell necklaces around the yard.

Games

403 Beach Volleyball: Set up a volleyball net or rope in the backyard and divide the players into two teams. Instead of using a volleyball, have the kids play the game with a large beach ball.

404 Surf's Up: Borrow a surfboard and set it on the ground. Have one player step up on it while the rest of the players sit around the board and gently move it in an effort to rock him or her off.

405 Hula-Do: Choose someone to be Hula Simon. Line the guests up in a row and have them respond to orders from Hula Simon, but only when he or she says 'Hula-Do'. Have all the commands relate to a hula dance. Be sure to make up your own wacky steps.

Sports and Games Parties

A perfect collection of parties for kids
with energy to burn.

Ages 2–8

Bazillions of Balloons Party

Have a blast with our Bazillions of Balloons Party. All you need are some inflated ideas, a little 'hot air', and a bazillion balloons! Then watch the kids as they try to bat, catch and pop the party fun.

Invitations

- Create big balloon invitations with party details that grow right before your eyes. Write party details on the surface of an inflated balloon using a permanent felt-tip pen in a contrasting colour. Deflate the balloon and watch the words shrink. Place the balloon in an envelope and mail it with instructions to blow up the balloon to read the message.
- Blow up balloons with air or helium and tie off the ends. Write party details on the surface, place balloons in individual boxes and hand deliver to guests.
- Write party details on a small piece of paper, roll the paper into a tube and insert it into a balloon. Blow up and tie off the balloon. Hand deliver to guests. The kids will have to pop the balloon to read the party invitation!

Balloon Cake

- Bake three round cakes in oven-proof bowls; cool.
- Decorate each cake a different colour, preferably red, blue, and yellow.
- Attach a licorice 'ribbon' to each cake
- Write a special message on top of each cake 'balloon'.

Variations

- Have a clown come to your party and ask him or her to make balloon creatures for all the kids.
- Have a clown come to the party to teach the kids how to make their own balloon animals.
- Plan a water balloon party, get parents' permission, and have the kids bring a set of extra clothes to the party.

Helpful Hints

- Be sure to supervise young children around balloons. Uninflated and popped balloons pose a choking hazard.
- Have lots of extra balloons on hand so when they pop the fun doesn't stop!
- Rent a helium tank from a party store to inflate the bazillion balloons easier.

Prizes and Party Bags

- Give the kids a balloon bouquet to take home. Attach regular balloons onto straws or tie helium balloons onto long ribbons.
- Send the kids home with a package of variously sized, uninflated balloons.
- Give the kids a pack of uninflated water balloons to enjoy in their own yard.
- Hand out long, thin balloons so the kids can make their own balloon animals at home. Enclose printed instructions for creating a simple balloon animal.

Costumes

- Have the kids use balloons to create a unique balloon costume to wear to the party. They might make hats or decorate their shoes with balloons, stuff their clothes with balloons or wear the balloons around their ankles and wrists. The kids can even use deflated balloons and glue them to an old vest, apron or tie. Award a prize—a bouquet of balloons—for Best Costume.

Decorations

- Decorate with balloons everywhere—the more the merrier. Tie balloons around the mail box, on the front yard trees, along the roof line, down the driveway or around the front door to greet your guests as they arrive.
- Fill the party room with balloons—attached to the door handles and along the walls, floating or suspended from the ceiling, for a balloon canopy.
- Cut out balloon shapes from coloured paper and use them as place mats, wall hangings and other decorations.

Games

406 Play Pop-a-Balloon. Tie a balloon around the ankle of each child and let the kids try to pop one another's balloons by stepping on them. The trick is to keep their own balloon from being popped by the other players.

407 Write challenges on small pieces of paper for each of the kids, such as 'Do a dance', 'Kiss a friend', 'Sing a song' or 'Do a somersault'. Stuff one note in each balloon, blow up balloons and toss them onto the party floor. Have the kids try to pop a balloon. When a balloon pops, everyone must stop moving. The guest who popped the balloon must read the instructions on the note and perform the challenge.

408 Play 'Who can keep the balloon up in the air the longest' or 'Who can pop the most balloons'.

409 Inflate some long, thin balloons and teach the kids how to make their own balloon animals. Instructions are available at a library or at party stores.

410 Give the kids felt-tip pens, stickers and other decorations so they can detail their balloon animals. Then add paper cut-outs for arms and hands, legs and feet, ears and hair.

Ages 4–8

Balloon Blast

It's an all-balloon party at this Balloon Blast. The party begins with balloons and ends with balloons—and has billions of balloons in between. All you need is a little hot air!

Invitations

- Blow up a balloon and pinch the end. Write party details on the balloon using a felt-tip pen. Repeat for each guest. Deflate the balloons, insert in envelopes and mail. The guests will have to blow up the balloons to read the party details.

- Write the party details on small squares of coloured paper and roll into thin tubes. Insert tubes into balloons and blow up balloons. Hand deliver or mail in boxes to guests. They'll have to pop the balloons to read the details.

- Buy a helium balloon for each guest and write the party details on a small sheet of paper. Punch a hole in the paper and attach by string to the balloon. Tie balloons to the doorknobs or letter boxes of guests.

- Make balloon invitations from paper. Fold paper in half and cut out ovals, being careful not to cut where the paper is folded; this will hold the two parts of the card together. Write the party details inside the cards. Attach a length of string. Mail to guests.

Balloon Cake

- Bake cake mixture in a well-greased, round, ovenproof bowl—a little longer than the baking instructions recommend. Insert toothpick to see if the cake is finished; if no mixture sticks to the toothpick the cake is ready.

- Remove cake from bowl and decorate with icing tinted to a favourite colour.

- Write any party details on the cake with piping bags. Make a string at the bottom of the cake with icing or licorice.

- Surround the Balloon Cake with balloon-shaped cupcakes.

Prizes and Party Bags

- Send the kids home with the balloon animals and balloon people they made.
- Give the guests a sack of deflated balloons to play with at home.
- Hand each guest a personalised balloon.

Costumes

- Ask the kids to use balloons in some creative way as part of their costume. One guest might tie inflated balloons to her shoes, another might make a tie out of deflated balloons and another might create an interesting balloon hat. Have them wear the balloon accessories to the party and award a prize for the Most Imaginative Costume.

Decorations

- Tie a balloon to every tree, shrub, fence post and anything else in your yard.
- Use helium balloons tied together to make archways or canopies.
- Make balloon animals and set them on the table as a centrepiece.

Variation
- Have a Bubble Party instead of a Balloon Party and make bubble-blowing the theme for your invitations, food, games, and prizes.

Helpful Hint
- Balloons can be dangerous so watch the kids as they play. If anyone is afraid of the loud noises when the balloons pop, provide ear plugs so they can still enjoy the fun.

Games

411 Air Balloon: Give each guest a large balloon and have everyone stand in a circle. On the word 'Go' have the guests hit their balloons into the air. Every time a balloon gets near a kid, he or she must hit it into the air again. If a balloon touches the ground, the kid nearest that balloon is out. Award a prize to the last player.

412 Balloon Bounce: For a variation on Air Balloon, have the players keep the balloons up in the air using only their heads—or feet!

413 Balloon Stunts: Write a number of body stunts or tricks on small pieces of paper, such as 'Jump on one foot', 'Walk backwards', 'Do a funny dance' and so on. Have each player draw a piece of paper from a hat and follow the instructions while trying to keep his or her balloon up in the air!

414 Cement Shoes: Have the players try to keep their balloons up in the air without moving from the spot where they stand.

415 Tennis Balloon: Give the players tennis rackets and have them pair up. Let them bat a balloon back and forth over a net, table or fence. Players score one point if the balloon hits the ground on their opponent's side of the net.

416 Volley Balloon: Divide the group into two teams on either side of a volleyball net. Have them play volleyball with a balloon.

Ages 5–14

Bike and Trike Party

For a wild wheelie party, have the kids bring their bikes and trikes to ride for a couple of hours. Then watch the party really start to roll.

Invitations

- Cut out pictures of trikes and bikes from toy catalogues and glue them on the front of folded sheets of paper. Draw a path from the bike to the inside of the card. Have the path lead to a picture of your home. Write the party details next to the picture.

- Cut out a picture of a bike and reproduce it on coloured paper. Cut out the bikes and cut off the wheels. Cut out wheels from different-coloured paper, and attach to all bikes; use V-clips so the wheels move. Write the party details on the wheels; mail.

Bike Cake

- Bake two round cakes; cool.
- Set the cakes next to each other on a platter to form bike wheels.
- Attach a length of rectangular biscuits along the top to form a bike frame.
- Make handle bars out of two peeled bananas.
- Decorate cakes to look like giant wheels with spokes. Use cherries to anchor the spokes in the centre of each cake.

Variation

- Instead of a Bike and Trike Party, have a Wagon Party, a Wheelbarrow Party, a Skateboard Party or a Hot Wheels Party.

Helpful Hints

- While on parade be sure there is an adult in the back of the line as well as the front.
- Make sure everyone has a helmet before you begin the bike activities and parade.

Prizes and Party Bags

- Give the kids bike accessories to take home; some ideas are horns, reflectors, bike stickers, streamers, bike seat covers, mirrors, bike helmets or small personalised licence plates.

Costumes

- Have the kids come dressed in biking shoes and brightly coloured bike-racing clothes, such as stretch shorts and tops.

Decorations

- Instead of decorating the party room, decorate the bikes and make that part of activity time. When the kids arrive with their bikes set the bikes up on the front lawn or backyard patio. Then let the kids decorate them with crepe paper, streamers, decals, stickers, horns, reflector tape, flags, windmills and noise-makers. Provide tape, string and scissors to complete the decorating fun and have the kids attach the stickers and decals with tape, if you don't want them to be permanent. (You may want to ask the kids' parents regarding permanent decorations.)

- Let the kids decorate their bike helmets, too.

Games

417 After the kids decorate their bikes, blindfold a selected player. Have the rest of the group mix up the bikes. The blindfolded player must try to guess which bike is his or hers just by feeling—and without wrecking all the decorations!

418 Make an obstacle course for the kids to manoeuvre on their bikes. Award prizes for completion and timing, or award individual points for each stunt along the way.

419 When everyone finishes decorating their bike or trike, it's time for a parade. Plan a safe route for your bike brigade and choose a mature leader to guide the group. Move along the sidewalks and pathways slowly and head for a destination, such as a park, where the kids can ride around freely, or an ice-cream parlour, where the kids can have dessert. Award prizes for the decorated bikes and be sure everyone gets a prize. Have awards for Most Creative, Silliest, Strangest, Scariest, Most Likely to Come Apart, Most Covered with Decorations and Most Colourful.

Ages 6–10

Backyard Bowling

The kids will be bowled over by this Backyard Bowling party—and they won't even need real bowling balls! Any ball will do, as long as the kids have something fun to knock over. Get ready for a striking good time!

Invitations

- To make bowling ball invitations, fold sheets of black paper in half and cut out circles. Be sure not to cut the edge of the circle where the paper is folded; this will hold the two parts of the card together. Decorate the tops of the round cards with three small white circles. Open the cards and write the party details inside using white or silver ink.

- Cut out several bowling pins from white paper. Draw stripes on the necks of the pins using a felt-tip pen. Write a few of the party details on one pin, more details on the next pin and so on. Stick the pins in envelopes and mail to the guests. When the guests open the envelopes and pour out the pins they'll have to piece the information together to figure out what it says.

Variation
- Take the kids to a bowling alley and let them play a real game.

Helpful Hints
- Save those squeezable plastic juice bottles—they make great bowling pins.
- Ask the local bowling alley if they have any old equipment they are willing to sell or lend for the party.

- Pick up some brochures at your local bowling alley, write the party details inside with a black felt-tip pen and mail to the guests.

Bowling Ball Cake

- Bake two chocolate cakes in round pans.
- Layer the cakes and decorate them with light-coloured icing.
- Draw alleys with black or chocolate tube icing.
- Top with tiny toy bowling pins or small white mints, set up in triangle formation and chocolate balls for bowling balls.

Prizes and Party Bags

- Let the bowlers keep their bowling shirts.
- Give each kid a personalised bowling pin to take home.
- Buy each guest a little bowling set, available at toy stores.

Costumes

- Ask the kids to wear funny bowling shirts they've created using puff paints or felt-tip pens and one of their parent's old shirts. Or provide the shirts, paints and pens for the kids and let them decorate the shirts at the party.

- Divide the guests into teams, then write each team's name and logo on T-shirts with felt-tip pens or puff paints. Give the shirts to the kids as they arrive.

Decorations

- Cut out giant bowling balls from black cardboard or paper and large pins from white paper. Write the names of the guests on the balls and pins, then mount them on the fence, the side of the house or on the backyard trees.

- Cut out and personalise paper bowling balls for place mats and set them on the party table. Buy some old pins from a bowling alley to use as decorations on the table. Personalise them and give them as take-home gifts at the end of the party.

- Make a giant scoreboard from poster board and mount it on the fence or wall. Keep score as the players knock down pins during the games.

Games

420 Batty Bowling: Find a number of silly or odd items that can be knocked over by a ball, such as a plastic milk carton, a candlestick, a stand-up doll, a plastic vase of flowers, a pizza box, a tower of empty cans, an umbrella stand, an empty cereal container and a book. Line them up like bowling pins and let the bowlers try to knock them over with volleyballs, tennis balls or golf balls.

421 Line Bowling: Instead of setting up the pins in a triangular pattern, set them up in a long row. Let one player roll a ball to knock over a pin. If the player is successful, let him or her go again. If not, the line is reset and the turn moves to another player. Whoever knocks them all over, one by one, wins.

422 Squirt Gun Bowling: Instead of a bowling ball, use a water gun. Make paper pins by cutting out small white paper triangles, folding them into cones and propping them up on a fence or table. Give each kid five seconds to squirt the pins over, then reset the pins and let the next kid go. Keep score. Whoever has the highest score after five rounds wins.

423 Domino Bowling: Buy a bunch of inexpensive dominoes and give equal amounts to all the guests. Have them spread out on the driveway and build a domino track by standing each domino upright close to one another. When everyone's finished, let one kid knock over the first domino as the other guests watch.

A Day at the Races

Spend a day at the races and let your kids test their luck—or skill—at winning a few challenging relay races. From the Big Foot Relay to the Stuff-It Race, this party offers something fun for everyone. On your mark, get set, go!

Invitations

- Write the party details on small toy batons using permanent felt-tip pens, then hand-deliver the batons or mail them in tubes to your party guests.

- Make your own racing flags using plastic cut into triangular shapes. Write the party details on the flags with a felt-tip pen.

- Draw a large stopwatch on white cardboard for each guest. Replace the clock numbers with the party details then cut out the stopwatch. Write 'On your mark, get set, go!' across the front in red and green lettering and mail to your guests.

Race Track Cake

- Bake a cake according to packet directions and cover it with chocolate icing.
- Draw oval lines on the cake with white icing to form a race track.
- Decorate the cake with small plastic racers and tiny racing flags.

Prizes and Party Bags

- Send guests home with trophies and prize ribbons.
- Give guests racing flags to put on their walls.
- Hand out the tiny toys from the cake.
- Give the guests game books, balls and balloons to take home.

Variation

- Instead of relay races, have the kids perform a series of stunts, such as balancing acts, ball tasks, skipping-rope games, hopscotch variations or tumbling tricks.

Helpful Hint

- Be sure to have lots of prizes on hand—for both winners and losers. The prizes don't have to be expensive, just fun. Red, white and blue prize ribbons are a great way to enhance self-esteem.
- Just for fun, have some extra prizes on hand for the kids that don't win.

Costumes

- Ask the kids to wear comfortable athletic clothes for the competition.
- Make racing shirts for the guests by writing their names and numbers with puff paints on inexpensive white T-shirts.

Decorations

- Decorate the yard with crepe paper ribbons, streamers and racing flags. Use yellow ribbon to indicate the start and finish lines. Hang cheering signs on the fence with slogans, such as 'Go!', 'You can do it!' and 'You're a Winner!'.

Games

424 Big Foot Relay: Ask the guests to bring two shoeboxes to the party. Tape the lids onto the boxes, then cut a three centimetre-wide and a ten centimetre-long slit in each top. Have the contestants slip their feet into the slits in the boxes and race.

425 Bowlegged Race: Ask each guest to bring a tennis ball, or provide one for each participant. Line the guests up, give them each one ball and have them hold the ball between their knees. The first kid to race to the finish line without dropping his or her ball wins.

426 Foot-to-Foot Race: Have the players line up at the starting line. Tell them they have to race to the finish line by placing one foot directly in front of the other, toe to heel. It'll be a challenge for the players to finish without losing their balance and falling!

427 Book Worm Relay: Line up the players and give each of them a book to balance on their heads—without using their hands. Have them race to the finish line. Any player who finishes without dropping the book gets to race again, this time with something more difficult to balance, such as a toy, a small plate, an egg and so on.

428 Pass-the-Hat Relay: Divide the players into teams and line them up. Give the first players on each team a hat and a stick. Have them pass the hat down the line of players, balancing the hat on the stick. If a player touches the hat with his or her hands, or drops the hat, the hat goes back to the beginning of the line and that team must start over. The first team to finish wins.

429 Spaghetti Mess: Create a twisting and turning maze using five metre lengths of yarn. (Have one piece of yarn for each pair of kids.) Wind each strand of yarn back and forth, over and under every other piece of yarn until you have a looping mess (try to avoid knotting the yarn). Then give each kid one end of the yarn. The object of the race is for the kids to wind their way along the yarn until they discover who is also holding on to their yarn. The first pair of kids to reach each other in the middle wins.

430 Stuff-It Race: Divide the players into teams of four or five. Select one member from each team to dress up in an oversized sweatshirt and pants. Have the remaining team members inflate 50 balloons and stuff them into the sweatshirt without popping the balloons. The first team to use up all the balloons wins.

431 Divide the kids into teams and have them come up with their own fun relay race.

Ages 6–12

Bouncing Balls

There isn't a kid on the planet who doesn't enjoy playing with a ball. Large or small, soft or firm, plain or colourful, balls provide hours of entertainment for kids of all ages. Start your party off with a bounce!

Invitations

- Cut out ball shapes from folded paper. Do not cut the edges of the balls where the paper is folded; this will hold the two parts of the cards together. Decorate outsides of cards with felt-tip pens, glitter, puff paints and stickers. Write party details inside.
- Purchase some small balls and write the party details on them using a permanent felt-tip pen. Place them in boxes and mail to guests.
- Blow up some inexpensive beach balls and write the party details on them using felt-tip pens. Deflate the balls and mail in large envelopes.

Big Ball Cake

- Mix batter according to packet directions.
- Bake a little longer than the recommended baking time.

- Flip cake onto a large platter. Sprinkle platter with green-tinted coconut to form the playing field.

- Decrate the cake to look like a favourite type of ball, such as a soccer ball, baseball, beachball and so on.

Variations

- Take the kids out to a ball game!
- Mix the balls and games—play volleyball with a football, basketball with a tennis ball, baseball with a soccer ball and football with a beachball.

Helpful Hint

- Keep a watchful eye so the kids don't get hurt with the balls.

Prizes and Party Bags

- Give the kids a variety of balls to take home, including a table tennis ball, tennis ball, golf ball, beach ball and a super-bouncing ball.

- Hand out souvenir balls to all the guests. Have them sign the balls, then pass them on, until all the guests have signed all the balls.

Costumes

- Ask the kids to attach balls to themselves in creative ways, such as tied to their shoes, hanging from their belt loops or worn as part of a hat.

- Suggest the kids dress as favourite sports players.

Decorations

- Cut out giant paper balls from large sheets of paper or poster board. Decorate balls to represent different sports, such as football, basketball, soccer, tennis and golf.

- Hang beach balls along the fence or place them around the yard.

- Make a centrepiece out of balls placed in a large bowl. You might include tennis balls, basketballs, footballs, volleyballs and so on.

- Make a silly centrepiece using other types of balls, such as popcorn balls, balls of yarn, sock balls, pompom balls, meatballs and so on.

- Cut out round place mats from paper and set them on the table. Personalise each one.

Games

432 Jai Alai: Give each player a small plastic bowl or box. Pair the players up in two rows facing each other, about a metre apart. Give each player in one row a tennis ball. Players must use their container to toss the ball to their partners, while their partners must try to catch the ball in their container. Each time the ball is successfully thrown and caught, move the players farther and farther apart. Any pair that drops their ball is out. Play until only one pair remains.

433 Name-It Ball: Have players form a circle. Give one player a rubber ball. That player selects a category, such as 'chocolate bars'. He or she then bounces the ball to another player in the circle, who must catch the ball, state an item from the category, such as 'Snickers' and keep the ball moving to the next player. If a player can't name an item, holds the ball too long, or repeats an item, he or she is out.

434 Pass 'N Catch: Form a circle. Give each player a different ball. On the word 'Go' all the kids throw their balls across the circle to another kid, while trying to catch a ball coming back.

435 Seven-Up: Give one child a rubber ball and have him or her bounce the ball seven times. In between each bounce he or she must do a stunt or trick, such as clap hands, duck down, spin around and so on.

436 Wacky Ball: Give each guest a table tennis ball and have him or her tape a coin to it. Then have the kids try to roll the balls from a starting line to a finish line.

Ages 7–12

Bike Trek

Grab the bikes and gather the gang for a rigorous road rally. Just follow the map, watch for special instructions, and hopefully you'll all meet up at the surprise destination!

Invitations

- Cut out pictures of cool bikes from toy catalogues or from bike shop brochures. Glue them onto the front of three-fold brochure-style paper and write the party details inside.
- Tape safety reflector stripes on the envelopes for a hot biker look.

Road Rally Cake

- Bake a cake and cover it with chocolate icing.
- Outline a path in white icing to simulate a bike path.
- Place tiny bicycles along the path, racing toward the finish line.
- Set a small plastic trophy at the end.

Prizes and Party Bags

- When you cut the cake, give the toy trophy to the winner of one of the races.
- Pass out the toy bikes to the rest of the gang.
- Offer the riders accessories for their bikes, such as horns, streamers, mirrors, personalised mini licence plates and so on.

Costumes

- Ask the kids to come dressed in loud, colourful biking shorts and tops—the wilder, the better.
- Provide white shirts for the bikers and let the kids decorate them with different colours of reflector tape.
- Provide racing shirts of the same colour for all the guests. Buy some iron-on letters and put the kids' last names on the backs of the shirts, along with racing numbers on both both sides.

Variations

- Write the directions on paper plates instead of on sheets of paper. Post the plates along the route so the bikers have to watch for the clues as they travel.
- Write cryptic clues instead of obvious directions and let the bikers decode the messages to follow the correct route. For example, you might write, 'Turn left at the next floral street' (Violet Street).

Helpful Hints

- Write or print the directions on clean sheets of paper and number them for clarity.
- Be sure to write down the final destination of the road rally in case some bikers get lost.

Decorations

- Provide decorations for the kids so they can brighten up their bikes before the road rally. Include such accessories as colourful reflector tape, decals, handlebar streamers, crepe paper, bells, horns, mini licence plates and sports cards to clip onto the spokes of the wheels.

- Write the bike trek instructions on decorative paper to make it more fun to read.

Games

437 Copycat Bike: Take turns having bikers lead the group on a follow-the-leader run.

438 Bike Circus: Let the kids carefully show off their bike tricks. The one who does the most dazzling tricks wins a prize. Have them teach each other the tricks, too.

439

Road Rally: Set up a course for players to follow using a map of the local neighbourhood or a nearby park. Several days before the event, follow the course on your bike and write down directions for the kids to follow. For example, you might write down, 'Turn left at the oak tree', 'Follow the path through the tunnel' or 'Turn right at the first path'. When the bikers arrive, pass out the directions and send them on their way. When all the bikers have finished the rally, award prizes in a variety of categories, such as 'First Biker to Arrive', 'Last Biker to Arrive', 'Most Exhausted-Looking Biker', 'Biker Who Got Lost the Most' and so on.

Ages 7–12

Tag Team

It takes teamwork to put on a good party and teamwork to have a great time at this party! Here are some games of tag that will keep your party moving all afternoon.

Invitations

- Write the party details on luggage tags to get your Tag Team party going. Mail to the guests.

- Make a finish line out of yellow crepe paper or ribbon, write the party details on it and mail to the guests in a large envelope.

- Create your own starting flags by cutting out squares of white fabric. Draw a large 'GO!' on one side and add party details around the edges. Attach a short stick and mail to the guests.

Octopus Cake

- Make a round cake and 64 mini cupcakes.

- Frost with green-tinted icing.

- Set eight cupcakes around the cake to begin the legs of the octopus. Add seven more cupcakes to each of the initial eight to finish the legs.

- Set two large marshmallows on the round cake to make the eyes. Colour the eyes with tube icing. Make a mouth out of red licorice. Sprinkle on colourful lollies for spots.

Variation
- Combine relay games with the tag games to create your own games.

Helpful Hint
- Change the teams around every now and then so the same players don't keep winning.

Prizes and Party Bags

- Give the kids pocket games to take home so they can keep playing.
- Buy inexpensive game books and send them home with the kids.
- Give the guests racing flags and let them keep their new T-shirts.

Costumes

- Ask the kids to wear racing clothes, athletic outfits or shorts and T-shirts so they can move quickly.
- Make T-shirts for two teams by using two different colours for background, such as red and blue. Draw on team names, such as 'Sharks' and 'Whales' and players' names with felt-tip pens or puff paints. Give the shirts to the kids when they arrive at the party.

Decorations

- Buy large sheets of cardboard or paper in a variety of colours or in the colours of the two teams. Write cheerleading slogans on the signs, such as 'Go Sharks!' or 'Whales Rule!' Hang them up around the yard.

- Set the table with paper and plastic plates and cups in the team colours. Make place mats in the shape of racing flags.

- Play sports music in the background.

Games

440 Bank Robber: Divide the group into two teams. Give a paper bag of gold coins to one player on each team and have the teams stand at opposite ends of the yard. On the word 'Go' the bag holders must try to keep anyone on the opposing team from touching their bag of gold coins. The bag holders can pass the bag to other players on their team, but if the bag is touched, the opposing team gets to eat one of the gold coins in the bag. The bag is then returned and the game continues until only one team has any gold coins left.

441 Grab the Loot: Divide the kids equally into two teams on opposite sides of the yard. Place a small prize—such as a chocolate bar or a pack of gum—in the middle of the yard between the two teams. Give the members of each team a number—one, two, three and so on—then repeat the same numbers for the other team. When the referee calls a number, the two players with that number must run to the centre of the field, try to grab the loot and run back without being caught by the other player. Continue to put out new pieces of loot and call new numbers. The team with the most loot at the end of the game wins.

442 Loose Goose: Have the players sit in a large circle, facing in toward the middle. Tape a feather or a piece of paper to the back of each player. Choose one player to be the goose. The goose walks around the outside of the circle and grabs the feather from one of the seated players. That player must jump up and try to run and tag the goose before the goose runs all the way around the circle and sits in the empty spot. If the player can't tag the goose, he or she becomes the goose.

443 Octopus Tag: One player is chosen as the octopus and must stand in between two lines of players on opposite sides of the yard. Players try to cross the yard to the other side without getting tagged by the octopus. If the octopus tags someone, he or she joins the octopus in the centre by holding hands. They continue to try to capture more players until everyone is part of the octopus.

444 Have the kids make their own racing flags. Give them squares of white cloth stapled to a stick. Let the kids design and colour their flags using felt-tip pens or puff paints.

Ages 7–12

Gopher Golf

Gopher Golf offers a twist on the conventional nine-hole golf game adults play—it's more creative, more challenging and lots more fun. Grab your caddy; it's time to tee off!

Invitations

- Buy second-hand golf balls from a golf shop or a local golf course and write the party details on the balls using permanent felt-tip pens. Hand deliver or place in small boxes or padded envelopes and mail.

- On paper, draw out a golf course. At each hole draw a triangular flag and write the party details in the flag. Colour the course green and mail to the guests.

Hole-in-one Cake

- Make a cake and decorate with green icing.
- Tint shredded coconut green with food colouring and sprinkle on the cake.
- Outline the golf course with chocolate piping bag.
- Stick small paper flags at the holes.
- Use mini marshmallows for golf balls.

Prizes and Party Bags

- Send the golfers home with a set of coloured golf balls and a handful of tees spray-painted gold.
- Get the kids a cartoon or humorous golf book.

Costumes

- Ask the golfers to wear imitations of traditional golf leisurewear—slacks, collared T-shirt and tennis shoes.
- Have the kids come dressed in athletic wear, sweats, shorts and T-shirts.
- Buy inexpensive golf-themed T-shirts and distribute to the players as they arrive.

Variation

- Take the golfers out to the greens and let them play nine holes of real golf or 18 holes of miniature golf.

Helpful Hint

- Have the kids stand back when golf clubs are swinging so no one gets hurt.

Decorations

- Set up the backyard to look like a golf course. Encircle grassy areas with rope to make the individual greens and use a gardener's bulb planter to make the holes. Stick flags in the ground at each hole. If you don't want to make holes in your yard, another option is to use tipped-over tin cans.
- Along the fence, hang posters of golfing greats, such as Tiger Woods and Greg Norman.
- Write the guests' names on golf tees and set on the table to mark places. Set out clubs and golf balls for a centrepiece.

Games

445 Blindman's Golf: Once you've set up a miniature golf course in the yard, have players divide into two- or foursomes and play—without looking. Each time they are about to strike the ball, they must close their eyes! For added fun, award prizes for the best scores.

446 Golf Challenge: Divide the group into two teams, then divide the yard in half. Have each team design a golf course for the other team. Tell the teams to be as creative as possible. When both teams have finished nine holes, each team plays the other team's course. Award a prize to the team that designs the best course.

447 Goofy Golf: In this game of miniature golf, the kids must be creative with the clubs, balls and holes. For example, at the first hole have the golfers use broomsticks to hit oranges onto plates. At the second hole, let the kids use cricket bats to hit walnuts into tipped-over shoes. Use your imagination and think up other ways to play Goofy Golf.

448 Peewee Golf: Set up a Peewee Golf course on the picnic table for a new challenge. Cover the table with a white sheet, and draw a course using green felt-tip pens. Use small cans or boxes tipped on their sides as holes. Give the players pencils and have them hit marbles along the course and into the holes.

449 Golf Ball Babies: Give each guest a golf ball to decorate with permanent felt-tip pens. Encourage them to personalise their golf balls by drawing funny little golf faces.

Frisbee Party

A Frisbee Party? Why not! All you need is a big play area, a bright sunny day and lots and lots of frisbees. The kids can play games, have races, do stunts and tricks, all with their little plastic disks.

Invitations

- Buy tiny plastic frisbees from a toy shop, write the party details on them with a permanent felt-tip pen, and mail in padded envelopes to the guests.
- Cut out frisbee-sized circles from yellow posterboard, draw a sun on the front and write the party details on the back. Mail to guests in large envelopes.

Frisbee Cake

- Bake a round layer cake and decorate with white icing.
- Score the icing by dragging a fork around the top in circles to make the cake look like a frisbee.
- Copy the design and writing of one of the frisbees used at the party.

- Set colourful plastic mini frisbees around the outside of the cake for decoration.

Prizes and Party Bags

- Send the kids sailing home with all sizes, colours and designs of frisbees.

Costumes

- Ask the kids to incorporate mini frisbees with their outfits, such as make one a hat, attach another as a necklace and so on.

- Have the kids wear athletic clothes so they are comfortable while playing.

Decorations

- Buy a bunch of frisbees in a variety of colours. Hang from the fence, place them on the table and display them throughout the yard.
- Cut out paper frisbees from colourful paper and hang them around the yard.

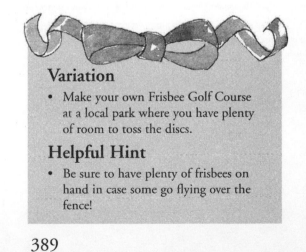

Variation
- Make your own Frisbee Golf Course at a local park where you have plenty of room to toss the discs.

Helpful Hint
- Be sure to have plenty of frisbees on hand in case some go flying over the fence!

389

Games

450 Frisbee Free-for-All: Gather the players in a circle and give each of them a frisbee. At the word 'Go' have them toss their frisbees across the circle to the opposite players, while trying to catch any frisbee that comes their way! The game is chaos, so it should be challenging and fun.

451 Frisbee Golf: Buy some inexpensive wicker baskets from the hobby store and attach a rope to each handle. Tie the baskets to various trees or other tall points so that the baskets hang about chest-high to the kids. Give all the kids frisbees and place them several metres from the starting basket. Each kid gets two chances to toss their frisbees into the basket; if a kid misses on the first throw, he or she throws again from wherever the frisbee landed. Each player gets one point for each basket he or she makes. When all the players have had their two throws, the whole group moves to the next basket and tries again. Whoever gets the most points wins.

452 Frisbee Hop: Line two teams up three metres apart and facing each other; each team's player should be a metre apart from their fellow teammates. Give every player—except for the first kid on each team—a flexible frisbee. The players without frisbees then stand at either end of the space between the teams. On the word 'Go' they must try to walk across the path while the players from the other team try to tag their feet with a low-flying frisbee toss. Anyone who is tagged is out. Repeat with all the players. The team that lasts the longest wins.

453 Frisbee Marathon: Divide the players into two-man teams; give one player on each team a frisbee. Have them stand ten metres apart, with plenty of space around. On the word 'Go' have the players toss the frisbee back and forth, in a competition. Any team that drops their frisbee is out. The last team left wins a prize.

Ages 8–12

Kite-flying Party

The next time someone tells you to
'Go fly a kite', throw a Kite-flying Party!
Your guests will love making and flying their
own one-of-a-kind kites. Up, up, and away!

Invitations

- Cut out tiny kites from paper, attach string with tiny
  bows for tails, and detail the kites with felt-tip pens.
  Write the party details on the backs and mail to
  guests.
- Cut off lengths of string about 90 centimetres long
  and six small pieces of fabric into rectangles the size
  of five-dollar notes. Write a few words of the party
  details on each piece of fabric. Tie the fabric to the
  strings, wind them up and stuff into envelopes. The
  guests must pull out the strings and untie the fabric
  from the kite tails to read the party instructions.
- Copy a photo of a child flying a kite and write the
  party details on the back. Mail to guests.
- Using origami books as instruction guides, fold the
  paper into kite shapes. Write the party details on the
  kites and mail to guests.

Kite Cake

- Bake a cake. Cut off the corners to make a diamond shape.

- Decorate the cake with white icing and make fun kite designs with tubes of coloured icing.

- Attach a length of licorice rope to make the tail.

Variation
- Take the kids to a park so they'll have plenty of room to fly their kites.

Helpful Hint
- Practise making and flying the kites first so you can teach the kids how to make their own kites and how to get them up in the air.

- If you prefer cover the cake with shredded coconut tinted green with food colouring to simulate grass. Attach tiny paper diamonds to stiff gardening or craft wire. Stick them into the cake and you have kites flying over a grassy field.

Prizes and Party Bags

- Give the kids inexpensive paper kites to take home.
- Offer the guests kite-making kits to try on their own.
- Give the guests books on how to make their own kites.

Costumes

- Ask the kids to come dressed as pilots, aviators, astronauts, parachuters, flight attendants and so on.
- Have the kids make feather hats and wear them at the party so they can pretend to be birds.

Decorations

- Buy inexpensive, colourful paper kites and set them along the fence or the walls of the house.
- Make some interesting kite tails using a variety of lightweight, printed fabrics.
- Draw a giant kite on a white paper tablecloth and let the kids colour it when they arrive.
- Hang kites overhead to make a kite canopy.
- Make tiny kites for place settings. Personalise them with the guests' names.

Games

454 Kite-Flying Adventure: Space the kids apart and let them raise their kites one at a time into the air. Or have a race and see who can get their kite flying first.

455 Kite Puzzle: Buy two paper kites and cut them into large-sized puzzle pieces. Mix up the pieces to each kite, then divide the kids into two teams and see which team can be the first to put their puzzle kite back together!

456 Kite Relay: Divide the group into two teams and line them up. Give the first player on each team a kite. On the word 'Go' the kite-holding players must race across the yard and back—with the kite flying about a metre in the air—then pass it off to the next player in line on his or her team. The first team to finish racing everyone wins a prize.

457 Kite Race: Give everyone equal amounts of string, then see who can raise their kites the highest in one minute. Determine the height by measuring the amount of string let out from the roll.

Ages 8–12

Olympic Gold

Go for gold with this back yard Olympic Gold party! Set up plenty of fun challenges, test the kids' skills, and let them win medals for their country. Let the games begin!

Invitations

- Cut out award ribbons from red, white and blue ribbon fabric. Attach a gold seal to the top, cut the bottom into an inverted V shape, and write the party details in a permanent felt-tip pen on the front of the ribbon. Mail to the guests.

- Collect pictures of former Olympic winners from sports magazines or trading cards, glue onto folded cards and write party details inside.

Three Medal Cake

- Bake three round cakes.
- Decorate with three different, bright coloured icings.
- Attach ribbons on top to simulate Olympic medals.

Prizes and Party Bags

- Send the kids home with ribbons and trophies.
- Give the kids posters of Olympic winners.
- Hand out chocolate gold coin 'medals'.

Costumes

- Ask the guests to come dressed in athletic outfits that are comfortable and flexible.
- Have the kids come dressed as their favourite Olympic medal winner.
- Have each kid come dressed as an athlete from a different country.

Decorations

- Buy small trophies to set on the table at each place setting. Use a large trophy as a centrepiece.
- Hang medals and prize ribbons from the fence and trees.

Variation
- Take the kids to a sporting event.

Helpful Hint
- Make sure everyone wins at some event so there are no losers.

- Buy or make a collection of country flags and hang them on the fence. Make place mats from flags of different countries and assign a country to each contestant.
- Hang Olympic posters on the walls and fences.

Games

458 Body Mechanics: Design a series of athletic events the contestants must perform, such as hopping on one foot ten times, walking ten steps backwards without looking, walking like a crab, skipping backwards, jumping over a hurdle, throwing a ball up in the air while turning around and catching it and so on. Award ribbons to the best athletes in each event.

459 Cross Step: Draw a three metre by three metre grid on the foothpath or patio with chalk. Have each player stand on a different square. One at a time, each contestant must move to a new square after crossing out the square he or she was formerly standing in. The trick is that the players cannot step into a square that is occupied or crossed out. If a player cannot move to a new square, he or she is out. The game continues until only one player is left.

460 Gymnastics: Set out a pad or mattress. Have the kids do stunts on the pad, such as somersaults, rolls, cartwheels, knee-walks, headstands, handstands and so on.

461 Obstacle Course: Set a series of obstacles and have the players run through them. Include such things as crawling through a tunnel, climbing over a table, wiggling under a carpet and so on. Award prizes to the kids who complete the course in the best times.

Ages 8–12

Silly Sports

How do you host a Silly Sports party?
Just take the kids' favourite games and give
them a twist. Any sport is bound to turn
out silly using a different type of ball, a
different course and a different set of rules!

Invitations

- Buy a packet of inexpensive sports cards. Write the
  party details on the backs of the cards and mail to
  the guests.

- Write the party details on mini frisbees and send
  them in padded envelopes to the guests.

- With a permanent felt-tip pen write the party
  information on table tennis balls. Stuff them in
  padded envelopes or small boxes and send to the
  guests.

- Make sports banners out of paper, write the party
  details on the front and mail to the guests.

Silly Sports Cake

- Bake a cake and decorate it with chocolate icing.

- Tint shredded coconut green with food colouring and sprinkle over the cake.

- Set up a silly game by placing football, soccer, baseball, and basketball plastic sports figures on the cake.

Variation
- Take the kids out to a real sports game.

Helpful Hint
- Be sure to supervise the kids at play, since they're trying new versions of favourite games and may be unsure of what to do.

Prizes and Party Bags

- Send the kids home with sports cards, jumpers, banners and other sports accessories.

- Give the guests the balls from the party.

Costumes

- Ask the kids to wear a sports shirt to the party.

- Have the guests wear comfortable clothes, athletic suits or T-shirts and shorts.

- Suggest the kids wear some kind of silly sports costume, such as a baseball hat with a football shirt, golf pants with a skateboard shirt or basketball shoes with a swimsuit.

Decorations

- Set out sports memorabilia around the playing field, the table and the fence and walls.
- Hang sports banners and make up silly sports slogans, such as 'Slam Dunk Table Tennis' and 'Crooked Croquet'.

Games

462 Weird Baseball: Play a game of baseball without baseballs! Substitute other items for the baseballs, such as tennis balls, table tennis balls, sponges, sock balls, soccer balls and beach balls. Alternate the balls constantly so that everyone has to hit a different type of ball!

463 Blindfold Basketball: Play a game of stunt basketball, such as 'Horse' or 'Around the World'. The twist is that each time the players shoot the ball, they must close their eyes!

464 Golf Pool: Play a game of pool using golf or table tennis balls, or play a game of golf using tennis or table tennis balls.

465 Hoops and Scoops: Play basketball set to dance music, so that the kids have to dribble and shoot the ball in time to the beats.

466 Super Soccer: Play a game of soccer using a tennis or beach ball.

Ages 8–12

Skate-away

Host a skating party in your
neighbourhood park or driveway and
let the kids show off their roller blading and
skateboarding skills. Teach them a few tricks,
play a few games and everyone will skate
away happy!

Invitations

- Buy pairs of long white shoelaces. Write the party
  details in felt-tip pen on the laces, tie them into
  bows and mail to the skaters.

- Cut out pictures of skates or skateboards and write
  the party details on top. Punch holes in the skates
  and lace them up with thin red or black licorice
  strings. For the skateboard, tape on round lollies for
  the wheels.

- Buy skateboard stickers at the sports store and
  include them with the party invitations.

Skateboard Cake

- Bake a cake. When cool, round the edges with a
  knife.

- Bake four cupcakes.

- Deocrate the cake and cupcakes with different coloured icing.

- Add skateboard decorations and details to the cake with tubes of icing, sprinkles and lollies.

Variation
- Take the kids to the skating rink or a skateboard park and let them practise their skills.

Helpful Hint
- Make sure everyone is well-padded so no one gets hurt.

- Slice the cupcake tops off and press them into the sides of the cake to make wheels.

For a skating cake, make a sheetcake, ice to resemble a rink and set small plastic skaters on top.

Prizes and Party Bags

- Give the kids skating stickers to take home.
- Offer skateboard shirts to keep.
- Hand out skating magazines to the guests.
- Give the kids wristbands and kneepads to take home.

Costumes

- Ask the kids to come dressed in skating outfits. Have them bring their kneepads, elbow pads, helmets and other accessories. Rent extra pads from a skating shop, if you prefer.
- Have the guests come dressed as skate-boarders with oversized pants and baggy shirts.

Decorations

- Hang posters of Olympic ice skaters around the skating area.
- Borrow old skates from the skating rink and set them around as props.
- Borrow vintage skateboards from older neighbourhood kids to use as props.
- Cut out pictures of skateboarders from skateboard magazines and hang them around the area.
- Place the plates of food on top of skateboards.
- Play upbeat skating music in the background.

Games

467 Skater's Olympics: Set up a series of obstacles for the skaters to manoeuvre around, such as a chair, a series of cones, through a large box, under a table and so on. Time the skaters as they go through the course one at a time. Award prizes to the skaters with the best times.

468 Skate Race: Divide the players into two teams lined up in two rows. On the word 'Go' have the first two players race from one side of the skating area to the other and back again, then tag the next players to continue the race. The team that finishes first wins.

Ages 8–14

Olympics Party

Let the young athletes flex their muscles
for a gold medal at your Olympics Party.
Set up the various events, put the
challengers through the hoops and watch
them all come up winners!

Invitations

- Invite the kids to your Olympics Party by awarding
  them their first gold medal! Cut out cardboard
  circles and cover them with gold foil or spray-paint
  them with gold paint. Attach a colourful ribbon so
  the kids can wear their medals around their necks.
  Write the party details in permanent felt-tip pen on
  one side of the medal. Write 'Winner' on the other
  side. Mail to the athletes.

Gold Medal Cake

- Bake two round layer cakes; cool.
- Tint white icing with yellow food colouring.
- Decorate one layer with the yellow icing; top it with
  the second layer.
- Cover the top layer with the yellow icing.

- Attach a large ribbon or length of fabric to make the medal's neckpiece.
- Write the words 'Happy Birthday, Winner!' across the top of the cake.
- Set tiny flags around the outside edge of the cake.

Prizes and Party Bags

- Send the athletes home with frisbees, balls, hula hoops, or other inexpensive sporting equipment.
- Give the kids pictures of famous athletes or sports-team banners, flags or T-shirts.

Variations
- Take the kids to a sporting event and enjoy live-action athletics. Cheer for your favourite team.
- Place five cent bets on who will win, who will the first goal/point and so on.

Helpful Hints
- Try to include some team games, or group games, so everyone wins.
- Be sure to have medals for all the kids so that everyone takes home a prize.

Costumes

- Have the kids dress in sweats, athletic outfits or their favourite sports attire.
- Dress the party helpers as referees, in black-and-white-striped T-shirts and matching shorts.

Decorations

- If you have any Olympic memorabilia, display it in the party room to set the mood.

- Hang up posters from around the world to give the party room an international atmosphere.
- Hang up posters of sporting events or favourite sports figures.
- Place sporting equipment on the party table as a centrepiece. Have fun by decorating the centrepiece with crutches, ice packs and so on.
- Fill the ceiling with helium balloons.
- Hang flags from other countries or states on the walls.
- Play Olympic music in the background to greet the guests.

Games

469 Create a series of challenging games for the competing athletes, using the Olympic Games as a model. Include a relay race, a high jump, a weight-lifting contest and a discus throw.

470 Organise a decathlon. Have the kids perform ten different sports during the party—such as running, jumping, dancing, skating, swimming, biking, bowling, table tennis playing, frisbee throwing and miniature golfing.

471 Have a Silly Olympics, with such silly stunts as pie eating, wheelbarrow racing, clothes changing, feather-in-a-spoon carrying, frisbee throwing, hula hoop passing or balloon popping.

Ice and Roller Skating Party

Skaters rule the party scene! Strap on the skates and head for the rinks for a rolling good time. Or set up your own rink at the park, playground or on the footpath and skate away!

Invitations

- Get a picture of the local rink and make photocopies for all the guests. Write the party details on the backs of the pictures and mail to the kids.
- Buy some long shoelaces—the kind found on skates—and write the party details down the sides; mail.
- Send skater stickers along with party invitations.

Skating Rink Cake

- Bake a cake; cool.
- Decorate the cake with white icing to make ice.
- Add little plastic skating figures available from cake decorating shops or a bakery.

- Write the name of the guest of honour in cursive script; attach a skater at the end of the name to make it look as though the skater just etched the message.

Prizes and Party Bags

Variations
- Have a teenager teach the kids to skateboard.
- Play a game of ice hockey!

Helpful Hints
- If the kids have differing levels of skating ability, have extra helpers on hand to give support, instruction or guidance.
- Don't forget the knee and elbow pads!

- Give the kids a free pass to the local skating rink so they can have another day of fun.
- Hand out Polaroid pictures of the kids skating as a surprise memento.
- Give the kids skater bumper stickers.

Costumes

- Have the kids come dressed as Olympic skaters with fancy outfits for the ice or roller rink.
- Make matching T-shirts for your skating crowd so you can keep track of your group at the rink. Create a name for your skating club and use that name to decorate the T-shirts.
- Have the kids decorate their own T-shirts with puff paints and glitter.
- Have the kids come to the party dressed as punk skaters.

Decorations

- You won't have to worry about decorations if you go to a rink—the place is ready to go. But if you rent a private room for the party, bring along balloons, crepe paper and other decorations and spiff up the place while the kids are skating.

- If you're at the park, playground or on the front footpath, add a few decorations to give your location a party atmosphere. For example, decorate the pavement with some foothpath chalk, which will wash away with a hose or the next rain.

Games

472 Ask at the ice or roller rinks about games and activities they provide.

473 If you are at a park or playground, play Musical Skates. Make a large circle using cardboard stars, using enough stars for all but one skater. Have the kids skate around the stars while a portable CD player plays music. When the music stops, the kids must race for a star. The player who doesn't find an empty star is out. Remove a star and play again. Repeat until only one player remains.

474 Try Follow the Leader. Have one player skate around the area anyway he or she likes, while the others follow. When two minutes are up, blow a whistle and have the leader touch another player. That skater becomes the new leader and he or she then leads the group in a creative skate.

475 Play Skate for Money. Stand on the edge of the rink or playground with a handful of play money. As the skaters circle the rink, on each round they must, without stopping, try to grab a 'dollar' from your extended hand. Set a time limit on the game and when the game is over, have the kids count how many dollars they made. Then let them spend the money on small prizes.

476 Bring along a CD of skating and dance activities and play them at the park or playground. For younger kids, try 'Hokey Pokey', 'London Bridge' and 'Ring around the Rosy'. For older kids, try a country line dance or a square dance.

477 Teach the kids one special skating trick, such as 'shoot the duck' (squatting down on one foot with the other leg extended), skating backwards, skating in pairs or skating connected in a long line.

Bugs, Bears and Storybook Parties

This collection of thrilling games is perfectly suited to little kids ready to party!

Ages 2–8

Storybook Party

Make your child's favourite storybook come alive by turning your party room into a 'Lion King' jungle, a 'Little Mermaid' lagoon or even a Dr Seuss playground. For older kids, use popular chapter books. Open the book and watch the party unfold!

Invitations

- Photocopy the cover of a favourite book and white-out the title. Replace the title with the name of your party theme, then add the party details around the edge.
- Make your own small storybook from paper and use it as an invitation.

Storybook Cake

- Bake two rectangular cakes; cool.
- Set the cakes side by side to look like an open book.
- Decorate both cakes with white icing.
- Write your party title and other inscriptions on the cakes with piping bags, to look like words on a page.
- Place a piece of licorice between the two cakes to form a bookmark.

Prizes and Party Bags

- Give each kid a children's paperback book to take home and enjoy.
- Laminate special homemade bookmarks, or buy some from a bookstore.

Costumes

- Ask the kids to come dressed as characters from their favourite books.

Decorations

- Check out a bunch of books from the library and set them all over the party room.

Variations

- Arrange a special story hour with your local children's librarian and take the kids to the library for an adventure with books.
- Help the kids get their own library cards if they haven't got one already.

Helpful Hint

- Teach the kids how to handle books carefully—especially library books—so they learn to appreciate them.

- Choose a favourite book. Use paper to reproduce items and scenes found in the book. For example, you might draw large trees for a jungle, fish from under the sea and so on.
- Ask the library for reading posters featuring books on famous people.

Games

478 Read the first lines of favourite stories, and have the kids guess the book.

479 Ask trivia questions about popular books, and have a two-team contest to guess the answers.

480 Hand out picture books, juvenile books or young adult books, one to each guest. Have the kids sit in a circle and read the first line of each book, one at a time, to form a funny new story.

481 Let the kids create their own storybooks. Supply the paper and writing materials, and give the kids some ideas if they get stuck.

482 Award prizes for costumes. Make sure everyone gets a prize by creating lots of winning categories, such as Cutest, Scariest, Funniest and Most Creative.

Ages 2–8

Beary Fun Picnic Party

For a Beary Fun Picnic Party, all you have to do is invite the bears! But you may want to let the kids come along, too, just for fun!

Invitations

- Biscuit bears make great edible invitations. Mix up your favourite gingerbread or biscuit recipe. Use a cookie cutter to cut the dough into teddy bear shapes. Bake according to recipe directions. While the biscuits are baking, write the party details on icy-pole sticks; you'll need one for each bear. When the biscuits are done, remove from heat and immediately insert an icy-pole stick into base of each bear to form biscuit pops; cool. Hand deliver to guests.

Teddy Bear Cake

- Bake two round cakes and seven cupcakes; cool.
- Set one round cake next to the other on a platter to form a bear's head and body.
- Place two cupcakes at the top for ears, two at the sides for arms and two at the bottom for legs.

- Cut the last cupcake in half, leaving the top intact, and set in centre of the head cake to make a nose. Let the kids munch on the bottom half.

- Cover all cakes and cupcakes with chocolate icing.

- Make fur with shredded coconut or chocolate sprinkles, add eyes with chocolate chips or tiny biscuits and make a mouth with red icing or red licorice.

Variations

- Instead of a Teddy Bear Party, have a Baby Doll Party or a Monster Party, and let the kids bring their favourite related toys.
- Have an adult friend rent a bear costume and make a surprise appearance at the party.
- Take a trip to the zoo to see the real bears.

Helpful Hints

- Have everyone bring a teddy bear to the party.
- If some of the kids do not have bears, have a Stuffed Animal Party, and let the kids bring any kind of stuffed toy.

Prizes and Party Bags

- Give the kids miniature teddy bears. You can find them at craft or toy stores.

- Offer the kids picture books about bears to read at home.

- Hand out bear stickers. They make good and inexpensive prizes.

- Send the kids home with little bags of lolly bears.

Costumes

- Have the kids come dressed as teddy bears.
- Tell the kids to use face paints to create their own bear look, or paint their faces at the party as an activity.
- Offer the kids headbands covered with brown fur and decorated with furry ears. Pin a large, brown, pompom tail onto each guest.

Decorations

- If you have a collection of teddy bears, get them out and make them special guests at your party. You can hang them from the ceiling, set them on the furniture, decorate the table with them or have them peek out from various places in the party room.
- Cut out lots of teddy bears from brown paper and place them all over the party room. Name each bear after a party guest and at activity time, let the kids dress and detail their namesakes.
- Have a giant teddy bear at the front door to greet the guests. Stuff Dad's old clothes with towels and place the 'body' on the front verandah or on a chair. Set a teddy bear inside the body so its head just sticks out. On the door near the bear, attach a sign that says, 'Welcome to a Beary Fun Party!'.

Games

483 Play Teddy Bear Tails. Give each kid a 'tail' cut from brown felt. Have the kids tuck the tails into the backs of their pants or shirts and sit in a circle on the floor. Choose someone to be the Teddy Bear, looking for his or her tail. Teddy Bear must walk around the outside of the circle, touching each child's back, until suddenly the Teddy Bear grabs one of the kids' tails! As the Teddy Bear runs around the outside of the circle and tries to come back to the open space, the tail-less player tries to catch the bear and get his or her tail back. If the tail-less player doesn't make it, he or she becomes the next Teddy Bear to look for a tail!

484 Give each kid a large paper teddy bear cut from brown paper. Let the kids decorate the bears to look like themselves, using paper, fabric, glue and pens. Let the kids make whatever they want using the teddy bear cut-outs; some ideas include bear monsters, bear superheroes or bear cartoon characters. Tape the decorated bears onto the wall until the party is over, then let the kids take their bears home.

485 Make miniature teddy bears using brown socks. Have the kids stuff the socks with newspaper, then tie off the head from the body with a ribbon. Use ribbons to tie off the ears, arms and legs. Let the kids add details with permanent black felt-tip pens.

486

Bears like honey, so make some honey dough the kids can play with and eat! Combine half a cup of smooth peanut butter with a quarter cup of honey and half a cup of instant nonfat dry milk. Mix until the mixture reaches dough-like consistency. Divide the dough among the guests and have them shape the dough into miniature teddy bears. Then let the kids decorate their bears with sultanas, nuts, seeds, coconut, chocolate chips and other goodies. Let them gobble up the bears when finished.

Ages 2–10

Lions, Tigers and Bears Party

Time to monkey around at a Lions, Tigers and Bears Party. Turn your party room into a real zoo! Invite the wild animals over for some animal-antics, and see if you can tame them before feeding time!

Invitations

- Welcome your guests to your home-made zoo with home-made cage invitations. Using borrowed snapshots, photocopy pictures of the invited guests. Cut out cards from black paper and fold them at the side. On the outside of the card cut out bars to make a cage. Place the picture of one of your guests on the inside of the card so they appear to be inside the cage when the card is closed. Write the party details in white ink on the inside of the card.

Zoo Cake

- Bake a rectangular cake; cool.
- Decorate the cake with chocolate icing.
- Sprinkle the cake with brown sugar to look like dirt.

- Set small plastic animals on the cake.
- Let each kid have an animal to take home.

Prizes and Party Bags

- Give the kids plastic animals to enjoy at home.
- Let the kids keep their animal masks.
- Hand out books about animals.
- Give each kid a small stuffed animal.
- Find recorded songs about animals and give them to the kids.
- Hand out posters featuring funny animals.

Variations
- Go to the local zoo and have a real zoo party!
- If you know someone with an exotic pet, such as a lizard, a ferret, or a parrot, have them bring it to the party.

Helpful Hint
- This party is better outdoors, where the 'wild animals' can run free, so set your cages outside if possible.

Costumes

- Have the kids come dressed as favourite zoo animals.
- Dress the kids up as animals when they arrive. Use large sheets of crepe paper to create the costumes.
- Have the kids create costumes for one another using crepe paper.
- Instead of costumes, make or buy animal masks or snouts for the kids to wear.

Decorations

- Make the party room look like a zoo, with cages cut from large cardboard boxes. Paint the boxes with poster paints, cut out the fronts to look like cages, and cut back openings for the 'animals' to enter. Label each cage with an animal type and wait for the creatures to come to the party.

- Decorate the party room with stuffed animals (have the kids bring stuffed animals to the party).

- Be sure to have a camera ready!

Games

487 Play Animal Noises. Write the names of animals or draw pictures of animals on individual cards. Some examples include lions, tigers, bears and so on. Pass the cards out to the kids as they sit in a circle. Have them make the sound representing the animal on their card. Have the other group members try to guess the animal.

488 Play a variation of Animal Noises. This time, act out the animal's walk, instead of imitating the animal's sound.

489 Play Pull My Tail. Stick cloth or paper animal tails onto the backs of each player with tape. Have the kids try to collect as many tails as they can from one another, while trying to keep their own tails. Whoever collects the most tails wins a prize.

490 Let the kids use face paints to create animals on each other's faces. Have some animal books handy to give the kids ideas.

491 Make necktie snakes. Have each kid bring a necktie, or provide neckties by shopping at a second-hand shop. Open the large end of the ties by pulling out the threads, then stuff the tie with polyester fibrefill, using rulers or sticks to push the stuffing deep into the ties. When the ties are stuffed, glue them closed using a glue-gun or sew them up. Glue on buttons or pompoms for eyes or use puff paints. Then glue or sew on red felt tongues.

492 Let the kids make individual animal pizza faces using English muffins as the heads. Offer condiments to use as decorations, then bake in the oven until hot and ready to eat.

Ages 2–10

Pets on Parade Party

Host an animal-themed party and treat the kids to an afternoon with their favourite dogs, cats, mice and guinea pigs! Have the kids bring their real pets to the party—if you've got the courage—or have them bring stuffed pets for a make-believe Pets on Parade Party.

Invitations

- Cut out pictures of dogs and cats and glue them onto home-made cards. Draw speech balloons and have the animals invite the kids and their pets to the party.
- Send a snapshot of your dog or cat to each child with the party details written on the back.
- Ask the kids to bring their stuffed animals (or real pets—as long as they're on leads!) to the party.

Dog Bone Cake

- Bake a loaf cake and four cupcakes; cool.
- Set two cupcakes on each end of the loaf to make a dog bone shape.

- Decorate the loaf and the cupcakes with chocolate icing.
- Write a dog biscuit logo across the top.

Prizes and Party Bags

- Give the kids anything for a pet: fur brushes, fancy collars or tags, chew toys, pet snacks and so on.
- Have the kids take home the dishes they decorated during the party.
- Give the kids small books about dogs, cats and other pets.

Variations

- Take the kids to a dog or cat show to see all the fancy breeds and fluffy tails.
- Go to a movie or rent a video that features an animal, such as a talking pig, an animated mouse or a cartoon bear.

Helpful Hint

- Ask the kids to bring their animals in cages so the cats and dogs don't fight or require lots of attention.

Costumes

- Tell the kids to come dressed as their favourite animals.
- Award prizes for creative costumes, with such categories as Cutest, Fuzziest, Funniest, Most Vicious-looking and so on. Make sure that everyone gets a prize.

Decorations

- Place stuffed animals around the room.
- Make animal-shaped balloons and hang them from the ceiling.
- Cut out pictures of animals and use the pictures to decorate the tablecloth, place settings and front door.
- Play animal songs or sounds for background music to welcome your guests.

Games

493 Play Animal Bingo. Draw one extra-large bingo card on cardboard. Draw a grid of squares and fill each square with the name or picture of an animal. Copy the bingo card onto sturdy paper, enough for all of the guests. On individually cut-up squares, write or draw the same animals. Hand out the Animal Bingo squares, call out the animals as you pick them from the card pile and have the kids set dog biscuits or cat treats onto the matching bingo squares. The first player to get five in a row across, down, or horizontally wins a pet toy!

494 Have the kids sit in a circle and make animal noises one at a time, while the other kids guess the animal.

495 Play Make-a-Critter. Fold a large sheet of white paper in half and then in half again. Unfold the paper and spread it out on the table. Give the kids crayons or felt-tip pens. Have one kid draw an animal head in the top rectangle of the paper. When the kid finishes, fold back the top rectangle so it's hidden from view, and only the three remaining rectangles show. Then pass the paper to the left and have that kid draw the body and arms of an animal in the next rectangle. Repeat, having the kids draw legs in the third rectangle and feet in the fourth rectangle. When they've finished, unfold the paper to see what new animal the kids have created. If you like, pass around more than one piece of paper at the same time, so the kids can create a whole bunch of new animals.

496 Give each kid a plastic dog/cat dish. Have them write their pets' names on the dishes and decorate them on the outside with permanent felt-tip markers, paint and other decorative materials. (Don't use glitter, though. If the pets use the dish, the glitter may come off and get onto the food.)

Ages 3–10

Bugs Are Beautiful Party

It's time to bug the kids with a Bugs Are Beautiful Party! Kids seem to be strangely attracted to little critters, so why not make that your party theme!

Invitations

- Buy large or small plastic bugs at a novelty or toy shop and super glue them to the party invitations or to plain white cards. Write the party details around the bugs and place the cards in envelopes. Drop a few more bugs into the bottoms of the envelopes for an added surprise and mail to guests.

- Create your own critters from black paper. Trace or draw bug shapes on black paper. Cut out the shapes and glue them onto sheets of white paper. Write details (names, origins, favourite foods) about each 'party bug' on the white paper, or use metallic paints and write on the bug cut-outs. Add party details and mail to future entomologists.

Wormy Dirt Cake

- Make a spice or white cake or cupcakes, adding sultanas to the cake batter; cool.

- Decorate the cake with chocolate icing.
- Sprinkle crushed chocolate wafer biscuits on the icing to look like dirt.
- Add lolly worms and other lolly bugs to the dirt.
- Tell the kids to watch for bugs inside the cake, too!

Prizes and Party Bugs

Variations

- Go on a hike and have the kids find bugs along the way. When you locate a new bug, look it up in your guidebook to identify it.
- Have a picnic when you reach your destination, but try not to eat any ants!

Helpful Hints

- Be sure to tell the kids when the bugs are plastic and non-edible and when they can eat the food bugs!
- Don't put plastic bugs inside anything the kids might eat.
- Keep an eye out for non-friendly or poisonous insects.

- Send the entomologists home with a handful of plastic bugs.
- Give the kids bug boxes to use for studying insects in their backyard.
- Hand out books to help identify insects, or give the kids storybooks about bugs.

Costumes

- Ask the kids to come dressed as bugs! They can create costumes that replicate their favourite bugs, or make up unique new species.
- Have the kids give their alter egos names, such as Bug Man, Caterpillar Kid, Worm Head and Scorpion Girl.

Decorations

- Fill the party room with plastic bugs, insects, worms, ants and other creepy and crawly things. Sprinkle plastic ants on the table, stick lolly snakes in the snack bowl, hang spiders from the ceiling and spread bugs all over the floor.

- Tuck some insects into a few surprise places to give the kids a little jolt when they reach for a napkin or sit in a chair.

Games

497 Have a bug race and see how many bugs the kids can spot in the back yard or park in five minutes. Draw sketches of bug types or give the kids bug charts to help them identify the bugs they find.

498 Have the kids collect bugs. Give them bug boxes to hold their specimens and see how many bugs the kids can collect in a set time. Have the kids return the bugs to the yard when the game is over.

499 Play Caterpillar. Have all the guests stand in a line, bend over and hold onto the guest in front of them. Then have the first player in line lead the rest of the 'body' in a game of follow the leader. Give each player a chance to be the 'head' of the caterpillar and lead the body up, down and around the yard.

500 Make Refrigerator Bug Magnets. Spread out a newspaper on the party table. Place bug-making materials on the table, including small pom-poms, felt, wiggly eyes, pipe cleaners, feathers and other art accessories available at craft or toy stores. Have the kids cut out felt shapes to use as foundations for their bugs. Then have them glue on pompom bodies and heads, wiggly eyes and other details. Suggest that the kids make ladybugs, beetles, worms, caterpillars or create a strange new species. When the bugs are complete, give each guest a strip of magnetic tape (available at craft and hardware stores) cut to fit the length of the felt foundation. Peel off the paper and stick the magnetic strip to the bottom of the bug. When the bugs are finished, watch them magically stick to the refrigerator!

501 Have a Snail Paint. Find snails in the yard and let the kids paint them with non-toxic paints. Have a race with the decorated snails, then return the snails to the yard when they're all tuckered out.